RESTORING THE SUN

Joe Sutton

BROADWAY PLAY PUBLISHING INC
224 E 62nd St, NY, NY 10065
www.broadwayplaypub.com
info@broadwayplaypub.com

RESTORING THE SUN
© Copyright 2006 by Joe Sutton

First printing: June 2006
I S B N: 0-88145-296-3

Book design: Marie Donovan
Word processing: Microsoft Word
Typographic controls: Ventura Publisher
Typeface: Palatino
Printed and bound in the U S A

RESTORING THE SUN wasa commissioned by
The Sloan Project/Ensemble Studio Theater.

RESTORING THE SUN premiered on 22 March 2005
at the Cleveland Play House (Michael Bloom, Artistic
Director; Dean Gladden, Managing Director). The cast
and creative contributors were:

OTTO BOLTZMANN .... Geddeth Smith
LEN SPITZER .... Daniel Cantor
LAURA SCOTT .... Keira Naughton
PARKER STEVENS .... .Joseph Adams
ARTHUR DEWINDT .... Stephen Bradbury

Director .... .Connie Grappo
Scenery design .... Jim Youmans
Costume design .... Michael Krass
Lighting design .... Jack Mehler
Sound design .... Jim Swonger
Production stage manager .... Corrie Purdum

The East Coast Premiere of RESTORING THE SUN was presented by Contemporary Stage Company (Keith Powell, Producing Artistic Director) in Wilmington, Delaware on 1 June 2005. The cast and creative contributors were:

OTTO BOLTZMANN . . . . .Richard Easton
LEN SPITZER . . . . Greg Wood
LAURA SCOTT . . . . Lorca Simons
PARKER STEVENS . . . . Shawn Sturnick
ARTHUR DEWINDT . . . . Johnnie Hobbs, Jr

Director . . . . .Kent Paul
Scenery design . . . . Michael Schweikardt
Costume design . . . . .Nanzi Adzima
Lighting design . . . . Matthew McCarthy
Original music composition . . . . Robert Rees
Stage manager . . . . Joanne E McInerney
Production manager . . . . Sara J Tantillo

CHARACTERS & SETTING

OTTO BOLTZMANN, *an electrochemist, mid-sixties*
LEN SPITZER, *a "futurist" (business consultant), late thirties*
LAURA SCOTT, *a newspaper reporter, early thirties*
ARTHUR DEWINDT, *a university president, sixty*
PARKER STEVENS, *an electrochemist, late thirties*

In addition to the above, there is also a pair of voices, one a Congresswoman, the other an apartment dweller in France.

Place: Washington, DC

Time: 1989

An intermission follows Scene Four

Setting: A non-realistic unit set that allows for a variety of locations. There is also a slide projection system.

A note about the text (for the actors): A dash in the text (—) indicates an interrupted speech. An ellipsis (...) indicates that the speaker trails off.

AUTHOR'S NOTE

Approach staging this play as you would a play of
Shakespeare's. By that I mean avoid, at all costs,
unnecessary, naturalistic detail. Allow the restaurant
table to be the lab table; that's quite all right. Above all,
preserve the play's drive and momentum. That's most
important.

to my sons

ACT ONE

PROLOGUE

(A lecture hall, filled with both students and faculty, is buzzing with excitement—when suddenly a schematic drawing of an electrolytic cell is projected onto a large white screen. [A drawing of this electrolytic cell, hereafter referred to as the "cell", can be found in the back of this book.] In front of this screen stands OTTO BOLTZMANN, *staring out imposingly, speaking, when he does, in a voice that is both heavily accented [part British, part central European], and magnificently, magnetically commanding. The crowd instantly quiets.)*

BOLTZMANN: Electrochemistry requires two things, a cathode and an anode. *(He takes a step towards the audience.)* Between these two is the electrolyte, a fluid in our case, which conducts the current from one pole... to the next. *(He now he takes another step, a look of barely contained excitement animating his face.)* It is there, at this second pole that a reaction occurs which has...well, let's just say it's caused a bit of a stir. And what IS this reaction? Well, the first aspect of the reaction is the production of a special kind of atom called a deuterium atom. These attach to... *(He spins around quickly, pointing at someone.)* ...just making sure you're all listening. *(Adding then, impishly)* Are you? *(Then, resuming)* Once the deuterium is at the surface of the metal, the surface of the cathode, a second, truly ASTONISHING reaction occurs...the deuterium begins to absorb WITHIN the

cathode. It is almost as if a door has opened into a
house with many rooms. And into these rooms comes
an ever increasing number of guests—deuterium
atoms, if you will—who squeeze closer and closer
together. And to make things more interesting, these
deuterium atoms begin to give off their electrons until
finally a truly miraculous reaction occurs. They begin
to join together. In other words, due to the compression
that is occurring within this household—a household
from which these guests can never escape, there is
the possibility of enough collisions occurring in the
hallways that the guests, some of them anyway,
will actually begin to fuse together and become one.
And the upshot is we have heat. With each collision
a small bit of heat is generated, until, at the end, after
BILLIONS of such collisions, we can actually boil a cup
of water! Isn't that amazing? What do you think? *(Slight
pause)* Do you understand? I don't get the sense you
understand. Think for a second of a cup of water. Are
you visualizing a cup of water? It can power a car for a
year. It can power a car for a year! The entire country
could run for a decade on the water you could find in
a lake! We will no longer have a need for fossil fuels.
ANY fossil fuels. We will free mankind...with this
discovery we will free mankind from the constraints
of oil exploration. We will no longer fight WARS!
Regional wars, local wars, WORLD wars...over the
globalization of resources. Our entire society, our entire
WORLD...will be free of its worst impulses...and open
to its best. And all...because of this. *(And here again,
as he has before, he turns back to the enormous drawing.
Only to return to his audience, moments later, now a bit
self-consciously, wondering if perhaps his speech may have
seemed a bit grand.)* Anyway, that's...what I'm going to
say. After that press conference I... *(He then stop himself,
not wanting to remind them of the press conference.)* When
we arrive in Washington, tomorrow, that...will be my

testimony. *(Shoulders back, playful, he then steps forward again, eager to engage.)* And now, please, your questions.

(He then points—and the stage goes instantly dark.)

(End Prologue)

Scene One

(Moments later, lights up, it is now Tuesday at noon. LAURA SCOTT and LEONARD SPITZER stand in spotlights. They are talking on the phone. They are both breathless, speaking quickly.)

LEN: It's the worst thing they could have done.

LAURA: What's the worst thing they could have done?

LEN: Holding that press conference.

LAURA: Then why did they hold it?

(The lights then come up on BOLTZMANN, and LEN turns to him, not acknowledging BOLTZMANN's reticence.)

LEN: Why did you hold it?

BOLTZMANN: We felt pressured.

LEN: They felt pressured.

LAURA: By whom?

LEN: *(Back to BOLTZMANN)* By whom?

BOLTZMANN: *(A bit grudging)* There was another group doing similar research. We felt they might get there first.

LAURA: But why hold a press conference? Why not just publish first?

BOLTZMANN: We *did* publish first.

LEN: They *did* publish first.

LAURA: *(Aggressive)* Then why hold the press conference?

(Slight pause)

BOLTZMANN: *(Uneasy)* It wasn't my idea. I... I was against it.

LEN: Boltzmann was against it.

BOLTZMANN: It was felt... *(Stopping, uncomfortable)*

LEN: It was about money if you want to be crass about it. Patent protection. Isn't that right?

BOLTZMANN: That's right.

LEN: The University...well, you tell it.

BOLTZMANN: The University felt we had to protect our position. Their position. If it turned out there was...a windfall...they wanted to get their share.

LAURA: *(Suddenly understanding)* And the news conference was to stake a public claim.

LEN: Exactly.

LAURA: From then on, no one would be confused...the "University" was where cold fusion had been born.

LEN: Yes.

LAURA: *(Beat)* O K.

LEN: So you'll do it?

LAURA: Len, no, I didn't say that. I said...

(Suddenly the lights change, and LEN and LAURA are now in a restaurant.)

LEN: What?

LAURA: First of all, I have no idea what "it" is. Do what?

(LEN gestures for LAURA to take a seat. He is bursting with excitement.)

LEN: Be available to me. Be a resource. You may not have guessed it but I have no idea what I'm talking about here. I have to know more than I do.

LAURA: You want me to do your research?

LEN: Do my research... *(Then, adding)* ...be available to me.

LAURA: What do you mean, "be available to you?"

LEN: There are going to be stories. By tomorrow afternoon we'll be going before Congress. We'll be asking for money. There are going to be conferences coming up, two conferences. Each of these is going to generate stories. I'd like some of them to be positive.

LAURA: You... *(Confused)* ...you're talking about my newspaper?

(By now LEN too is sitting. He leans forward.)

LEN: Somebody is going to get the inside scoop. I'd like it to be you.

LAURA: Wait a minute, let me be clear on this. You're talking about my newspaper...planting stories... *(Suddenly outraged)* ...through me?!?

LEN: I'm not talking about anything unethical, Laura. I'm talking about making an arrangement. *You* get the story.

LAURA: I'm not the science writer.

(She looks at LEN angrily, waiting for him to respond.)

LAURA: Len, I'm not the science writer!

LEN: You took chemistry in college.

LAURA: I majored in chemistry in college. That's not the point!

LEN: What's the point?

LAURA: The point... *(She takes a brief moment, gathering herself, then)* ...all right, look, say you're right. We have a relationship. Don't you think *that's* a problem?

LEN: In what way?

LAURA: As far as credibility!

LEN: Laura, I'm not asking you to do anything wrong. I'm asking you to be available! When we have a response. When we have something that needs to get out, a part of the story that needs to be told, I'd like to do it through you. Is that really a problem?

LAURA: *(Beat, reluctant)* No.

(Beat. LEN is annoyed.)

LEN: Christ, you'd think you'd never done this before.

LAURA: I've never done it with a boyfriend before.

LEN: *(Snapping, childish))* We're not...Laura, I'm not your boyfriend.

LAURA: We have a relationship.

LEN: I'm not your boyfriend. *(Then)* By the way, I'm sorry I didn't call you last week.

LAURA: Uh-huh.

LEN: I was doing this!

(Beat)

LAURA: Let's get back to the story.

LEN: Let's order first. *(He picks up the menu. He quickly scans it. He then looks over at her. Light)* Come on, let's... *(He returns to the menu.)* They're supposed to have some really good fish.

(Finally she picks up the menu. Then, almost immediately, she looks over it.)

LAURA: Then what are you?

LEN: What?

LAURA: If you're not my boyfriend, what are you?

LEN: We haven't...I didn't think we were going out with each other...alone.

(He waits for her to respond. She doesn't.)

LEN: When I think boyfriend, I think...that's... *(Finally, exasperated)* ...what do you want me to say?

LAURA: How you think of yourself. In relation to me.

LEN: We have a relationship. *(He considers this a moment. then, comfortable)* I'll accept that.

(They stare at each other a moment.)

LAURA: Well, that's a problem. Even that's a problem.

LEN: In relation to what?

LAURA: This story. This...set of stories. *(Growing flustered)* Whatever it is you're giving me here.
If I'm going to publish and my name is attached,
and your name is involved...there are plenty of people who can connect us.

LEN: You continue to have the wrong idea of what I'm talking about. I don't *care* if they connect us. We're not doing anything wrong!

(Again they lock eyes—until finally LAURA looks down at the menu. Then...)

LAURA: I'm just—

LEN: Laura, please, just...look at the menu.

(And again she looks down. And another moment passes. When next she speaks her eyes remain down.)

LAURA: I know how you are.

LEN: What?

LAURA: On a story like this.

LEN: What do you mean???

LAURA: You "play" the writer. *(She looks up at him)*
You're going to play me.

LEN: Laura, listen to me. Put down the menu and listen
to me.

*(And this time, whether it is the intensity in his voice or the
look in his eye, something causes her to listen differently.
And she is rapt.)*

LEN: Do you understand what this story is about? There
is no more abundant resource in the world than water.
If they're right, if they can get energy from water...then
every resource we currently count on—oil, uranium,
gas, coal, become worthless. And there will be plenty of
people who will be very upset by that. *(Beat)* Now—

LAURA: What do you mean "if"?

LEN: What?

LAURA: You say "If they're right." "If they can get
energy." What do you mean?

(LEN debates how to answer. Then...)

LEN: I shouldn't have said "if". They *are* right. They
simply haven't gotten confirmation yet. And until they
do, until... *(Suddenly, impassioned)* ...it's a question of
integrity. Until they *get* confirmation, the two have
asked that I refrain from statements that are overly
definitive. But! And this is important. These are two
of the finest scientists in the world. Otto Boltzmann,
in particular, is a Fellow of the Royal Society. He
doesn't make mistakes. What he has done, what *they*
have done...is to set the world on its head; and that
has made enemies. And so they're gunning for us.

(Beat)

LEN: And so, in response...we're trying to be careful in
what we say.

(Beat)

LAURA: Let me—

LEN: Laura! *(This last he says a bit sharply.)*

LEN: Look, I'm sorry. I know you have questions; and I have questions. But can we eat first? And then we'll get back to them?

LAURA: *(Put off)* Sure.

(He smiles. He then picks up his menu.)

LEN: So what are you having?

LAURA: The fish I guess. *(She starts to pick up her menu, only to suddenly put it down)* Actually, can I just ask one thing? When you say confirmation, what do you mean exactly?

LEN: Another group getting their results. And so far that hasn't been easy. I mean, this isn't Newton we're talking about. This isn't an apple falling on your head. This is sub-atomic particle physics without the benefit of a theory. And see, that's the amazing thing with this. They have no theory here. They don't know *why* this is doing what it is, they just know that it is. But the problem is that without a theory they can't get other people to get their results. All they can do is give them the procedures, the materials, and tell them what to look for. But they can't find it for them.

LAURA: And what have other people seen?

LEN: Nothing. Actually, that's not true. They've seen alot. The problem is they haven't seen it together. One group's seen this, another group's seen that. The first group *retracts* their finding; now, they *didn't* see what they said they did. I mean, it's been an incredibly frustrating few weeks here. But the problem is we can't afford to wait. I mean, already we think the Japanese are moving on this, the Russians, the Indians. The

implications of this technology are so...insane...that we
have to move ahead with it. We can't afford to wait.
And so that's...why we're going to Congress.

LAURA: And your guys?

LEN: What?

LAURA: Your guys. What—

LEN: Laura, look, let's EAT first. I... *(Then, after a beat)*
O K, look, I can't talk about anything else. What else
do you want to know?

LAURA: I—

LEN: *(Excited, bursting)* Laura, look, I'm telling you, this
thing is gonna be huge. This thing, if it's real, is gonna
be HUGE! You know? It'll change the wealth of the
world! The countries that are rich will be poor. The
countries that are poor will be rich. And not just third
world countries. Our country. I mean, what will
happen with Detroit? Right? What will...and maybe
everything will be better. Maybe... It's just it's hard to
get a handle on what will happen. *(Beat)* I just know it
will be big.

(Beat)

LAURA: And you want...I mean, again, what do you
want from me? Exactly?

LEN: Look, I don't want you to be uncomfortable. O K?
More than anything...

(LAURA laughs)

LEN: What? *(Then)* Why are you laughing?

LAURA: Because you're Len Spitzer. That's why. I mean,
Christ, Len, it's not just the boyfriend thing. You're Len
Spitzer!

LEN: So?

LAURA: So...you make waves. You know? You're known! You...

LEN: Laura, look, this is not about me, O K? This is about them. I'm...I'm just a cog.

LAURA: You're *never* just a cog. *(She eyes him warily)* Never. *(Beat. And still she looks at him. Then...)*

LAURA: I'm trying to think how this would work.

LEN: Talk to your editor. See what he can arrange.

LAURA: Who, Heffler?

LEN: Yeah. See what he can arrange.

LAURA: He won't let me do it.

LEN: Why, what's he going to say?

LAURA: He's going to say "let Hensley do it," the science guy.

LEN: Tell him I won't talk to Hensley. Tell him I'll only talk to you. Because that's the truth, Laura. I have no reason to go to your paper except for you. I have a relationship with *you*. I trust *you*. I don't know or trust Hensley. *(Another pause)* Also, another thing, this is a two-way street here. I mean, yes, I'm coming to you for a favor, but I'm also coming to you with the biggest science story of the year; of the decade. There are people, and I'm not exaggerating when I say this, there are people who consider this story to be bigger than Einstein. Bigger than relativity. That's the kind... *(Suddenly, turning on a dime, pulling away)* But you know what? Never mind. I don't want to talk you into this. If...I don't want to talk you into this. *(He shoves away from the table.)* Let's drop it.

LAURA: Oh, right.

LEN: What?

LAURA: Like you're suddenly going to turn away. Like you're going to put all this time in...and then suddenly turn away. (*She is a little annoyed.*) Len, I told you, don't play me.

(*The two stare at each other for a long moment.*)

LAURA: I'll see what I can do.

(LEN *lifts his glass.*)

LEN: What more can I ask?

(LAURA *continues to stare at him.*)

LAURA: But Len, I'm serious. Don't play me.

(*And with that, she slowly lifts her glass—and they clink.*)

(*Blackout. End Scene One*)

Scene Two

(*Late that afternoon. The sitting room of a hotel suite.* BOLTZMANN *is joined by* ARTHUR DEWINDT, *a distinguished looking man in his sixties, and* PARKER STEVENS, *barely half* BOLTZMANN's *age. As the lights rise,* BOLTZMANN *and* STEVENS *are having an argument,* STEVENS *staring daggers at* BOLTZMANN.)

BOLTZMANN: Look, Len says—

STEVENS: I don't give a shit what Len says! Have some fucking balls, Otto!

(*And with that, he storms off, and* BOLTZMANN *looks after him. He is upset. He then turns to* DEWINDT *and a long moment passes.*)

BOLTZMANN: (*Then, fatigued*) Look, I'm not saying I disagree.

(*With that,* DEWINDT *quickly turns to the doorway.*)

DEWINDT: (*Calling out*) Did you hear that?

STEVENS: *(Off)* What?

DEWINDT: He's saying he doesn't disagree.

(STEVENS returns to the doorway.)

STEVENS: You don't disagree?

BOLTZMANN: No.

STEVENS: Then what are we talking about?

BOLTZMANN: It's a matter of nuance. I agree it should be mentioned. I don't think it should be emphasized.

STEVENS: It *has* to be emphasized. That's the whole point.

BOLTZMANN: I don't agree. *(Beat. His tone is getting angrier)* We are not in the business of generating nuclear products. We are in the business of generating heat.

STEVENS: Our critics will want to talk about products, Otto. They will want to talk about the absence of products.

DEWINDT: *(Interjecting)* Could you...I'm sorry, but could you...explain "products"?

BOLTZMANN: In physics—

STEVENS: Which we are not.

BOLTZMANN: *(Continuing, more angrily)* ...a reaction is expected to create not only the new element itself... but also its by-products! Deuterium fusion, for instance, is expected to create not only tritium or helium but also neutrons or gamma rays. Our experiment did not.

STEVENS: Which is what they will focus on.

BOLTZMANN: Which is why we should not. We should acknowledge it and then move on.

DEWINDT: I'm... *(He laughs.)* ...forgive me for interrupting again...but I don't understand. If—

BOLTZMANN: *(Furious)* Deuterium plus deuterium, that's D2 + D2...makes one of three things. *(He marches to the blackboard, writing it down.)* A tritium atom. *(He writes a "T")*

STEVENS: Oh, for—

BOLTZMANN: *(Overlapping)* A light helium atom. What we call He3. *(He writes an HE-3)*

STEVENS: We don't need a lecture, Otto!

BOLTZMANN: *(Overlapping)* Or regular Helium. *(He writes HE-4.)* In the case of the tritium atom, "T", a neutron is left free. So, too, in the case of Helium 3.

STEVENS: So—

BOLTZMANN: Now when this reaction is happening with billions of atoms there should in turn be billions of neutrons. A single reaction should leave billions of neutrons floating free in the lab. But it didn't. Why? Why are we still alive? Why have we been able to count no more than forty thousand neutrons coming out of our reaction?

STEVENS: Because it's a different reaction. It's a different branch. Each of these here is called branches. *(He points to* BOLTZMANN'S *drawing, singling out the three branches:)*

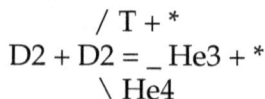

$$\begin{array}{l} / \text{ T} + {}^{*} \\ \text{D2} + \text{D2} = \_ \text{ He3} + {}^{*} \\ \backslash \text{ He4} \end{array}$$

[Lines = branches; * = neutrons]

STEVENS: *(Continuing, immediately)* We have found a new branch. And the question is "is it chemical?" And the answer is no. And why? Because of the heat. Because we have generated ten thousand times the heat we should have in a chemical reaction.

BOLTZMANN: And that's what we should say. We should talk about the heat.

STEVENS: Otto, we can't ignore the branches. We may eventually emphasize the heat, but we must *talk about* the branches. For one reason above all others. We have results! We *have* tritium. We *have* forty thousand neutrons. Where did these neutrons come from? They didn't just come out of thin air. There must be a reaction that has released these neutrons and we should discuss it.

BOLTZMANN: Go ahead! Please tell me where these neutrons have come from?

(His question, harshly challenging, leaves STEVENS *wordless.)*

STEVENS: I'm not saying we should go into details.

BOLTZMANN: You said "discuss". What does it mean to "discuss"?

STEVENS: I don't think we should overlook it. I don't think we should give it short shrift. *(Slight pause)* I don't think we should appear, or be MADE to appear, as if we are ignoring the question because our data are less than complete.

BOLTZMANN: *(Immediate, pissed)* Parker, may I stop you for a second, just for a second, and ask you a question? Have you EVER appeared before such a committee? Because I have. I have appeared before the committees of Parliament. I KNOW the questions we will be asked. And HOW we will be asked them. I know how we will look if we are introducing topics that we are not prepared to *discuss. (Slight beat, gathering himself)* I am not saying, I just said this two minutes ago, I am not saying we should not mention it. I am just saying our emphasis should be on the heat.

DEWINDT: You know, I...think you're both saying the same thing. If I may.

STEVENS: We are not saying the same thing. Otto is saying we should apologize and I am saying we should not.

DEWINDT: Perhaps—

BOLTZMANN: I am NOT saying we should apologize. I have NEVER said we should apologize. I am saying we have a wonderful opportunity and we should try not to squander it. *(Taking a moment, trying to calm himself)* For three weeks now the story has been out of our control. We have had to respond, or been pressured to respond, to concerns that are not of our choosing. Now, finally, we have the opportunity to—

(Suddenly the door flies open and LEN *appears. He is carrying a briefcase.)*

LEN: What's going on?

DEWINDT: We are in the midst of—

BOLTZMANN: *(Interrupting, impatient)* May I... answer please? We are sorting through what we are going to say and we have reached an impasse.

LEN: Oh?

BOLTZMANN: Leonard, I think it's important that we not appear defensive.

STEVENS: But that's precisely how we will appear!

BOLTZMANN: Parker wants us to talk about neutrons and gamma rays, which is not our strongest point, and I think we should concentrate on heat. What do you say?

LEN: I think we should talk about money. I think that's our strongest point.

BOLTZMANN: Leonard, please, be serious.

LEN: I am being serious. Fellas, you gotta understand what we're going into here. This is not a scientific conference. This is not a meeting of your peers. This is a

committee hearing of the United States Congress.
This is a bunch of guys, most of them barely literate,
who are going to decide whether or not you get the
money you want. And you know what? It's not fair.
It's not fair that people who will have no idea what
you're talking about are going to pass judgement about
your work. But that's the way it is. So what you have
to decide is if you're going to talk their language or not.
If you talk their language, they'll listen to you, they'll
give you a break, they'll probably give you what you
want. If you talk your language... *(A glint, an edge)*
...they will freeze you out. So what's it going to be?

BOLTZMANN: *(At a loss)* I...well, of course, you...

(LEN turns to STEVENS.)

STEVENS: I understand.

(LEN turns to DEWINDT.)

DEWINDT: I'm with you, Len.

LEN: Good. *(Beat)* Then let's talk about what's going on.
Where are we at the moment?

DEWINDT: Where—?

LEN: Have you talked with the chairman?

DEWINDT: *(Confused)* The...

LEN: The chairman. Of the committee!

DEWINDT: Oh. Yes.

LEN: And what did he say?

DEWINDT: *(Still confused)* I don't know; he was
impressed.

LEN: He said that?

DEWINDT: Yes.

LEN: And?

DEWINDT: *(Exasperated)* And what?

LEN: What else did he say?

DEWINDT: *(At a loss)* I—

LEN: Arthur, look, he's giving us cues here. He's... you're the President of the University. He's telling you what to be looking for. What did he say?

DEWINDT: *(Nervous)* He... *(Uncertain)* ...I don't know, outlined the way it would go...he thought. He would speak. Then...the minority member—

LEN: *(Jumping in)* And what would she say?

DEWINDT: What?

LEN: Did he say what Liz Kendle would say?

DEWINDT: No. *(Then)* Just—

LEN: *(Quickly, turning to the others)* What do you guys think? You were with her this morning. What was she like?

BOLTZMANN: Fine.

STEVENS: Nice.

BOLTZMANN: *(Overlapping)* "Impressed". I think. *(Turning, to DEWINDT)* To use your word.

LEN: Did she...was there anything on her mind?

(The two scientists look at each other.)

BOLTZMANN: Not—

STEVENS: She did... *(He stops himself.)*

LEN: What?

STEVENS: *(Worried)* She brought up the press conference.

LEN: What did she say?

STEVENS: She asked us about it. What we thought. If... *(Then)* ...how unusual it was.

LEN: And what did you say?

(Beat)

BOLTZMANN: That it's not what we wanted. That if we could have avoided it we would have.

DEWINDT: *(Defensive)* But we couldn't. I hope you made that clear. We had no choice in the matter.

BOLTZMANN: *(Hard)* That's what I told her.

LEN: And what did she say?

(Slight beat)

STEVENS: That she'd heard differently. She didn't go into details, but...it was clearly on her mind.

(Pause)

LEN: *(Quick, business-like)* All right, look, let's assume for a moment she brings it up tomorrow. What are you going to say then?

(The three men, BOLTZMANN, STEVENS, and DEWINDT look at each other.)

STEVENS: That—

DEWINDT: I think we should say what we agreed to. That we had no choice in the matter. That it *wasn't our* decision.

BOLTZMANN: *(Angry)* Of course, it was, Arthur. Whose decision was it?

DEWINDT: *(Hot)* Look, if you can't handle this question, I can! If you think you're going to have difficulty with this, give it to me!

LEN: And what will you say?

DEWINDT: That the science is only one part of it. That there are other issues as well. And the science, by the way, was not affected. We published in a reputable journal. We had and continue to have conversations throughout our community—

BOLTZMANN: But the issue—

DEWINDT: *(Loud)* I know what the issue is!

(Beat)

LEN: *(After a pause)* What's the issue?

(There is silence. Clearly this is something they've been fighting about a lot.)

BOLTZMANN: *(Seething)* The issue is how science is conducted. How its integrity is preserved. What happens when an advance, particularly a controversial advance, is rushed into the public arena. *(Adding, his voice low)* Circumventing the checks and balances that are built into the system.

LEN: What happens?

BOLTZMANN: What happens is what we've seen here. A feeding frenzy. A sense of distrust. An obligation to publish and support material without adequate work being done. We have been put in a very difficult position by the decisions that were made here.

STEVENS: And what would you have done differently? *(This last is said sharply.)*

BOLTZMANN: Wait.

DEWINDT: Until when?

BOLTZMANN: Until we were ready.

DEWINDT: And if Thornton published first?

BOLTZMANN: So be it.

(Beat)

STEVENS: Oh, well, that's ridiculous.

LEN: This is Gilbert Thornton?

DEWINDT: Yes.

LEN: And he was—

DEWINDT: Just tell me one thing, Otto. Why!
(Now he is furious.)

DEWINDT: Why should we let him get credit for
the work you two have done?

BOLTZMANN: Because—

DEWINDT: You see, that's the thing Otto doesn't
understand. *(Continuing, self-righteous, enraged)*
Certainly we would have preferred to publish first, to
not hold a news conference, but that wasn't possible.
We had a man...I don't want to impugn the man, but
we had a man at a rival institution, who came up with
nearly identical data on nearly identical subjects at the
very same time as we were conducting *ground* breaking
experiments! And we wondered how could this be?
How could two sets of scientists only sixty miles apart
be conducting the same set of experiments *when no one
else in the world has thought of them?* And you know
the answer? Because this man at this rival institution
was their reviewer, that's how! He had seen Otto
and Parker's work when they had submitted it to
the Department of Energy. And he had tailored his
research, research which until then had had NOTHING
to do with hydrogen fusion, to the questions they had
been asking. And then he took it a step further. He said
he had made a breakthrough. He said on the basis of
work he had done subsequently that he had made a
breakthrough and he was now going to publish it.
And we were left with a choice. We could either let
him go ahead and take credit for our work or we could
publish in front of him, and announce the whole thing
at a press conference. And that's what we did. *(Beat)*
And I have no apologies for it.

(Pause)

LEN: And he considered that a betrayal.

DEWINDT: *(Angry)* What?

LEN: He...I'm sorry, didn't you have an agreement with him?

(Beat)

BOLTZMANN: We did, yes.

LEN: To publish together.

STEVENS: To *submit* together.

DEWINDT: *(Irritated)* We were going to *submit* together to "Nature". They were going to decide whom to publish.

LEN: And you thought they might select him?

BOLTZMANN: Yes.

LEN: Why?

BOLTZMANN: He—

STEVENS: He's a physicist. This is fusion. It's a slam dunk.

LEN: Still—

STEVENS: No "still", Leonard. That's it.

LEN: That's—

STEVENS: Leonard, look, for fifty years this has been the province of physics. Physicists made the H bomb, physicists made the nuclear reactors. They are not *about* to allow chemists...let alone ELECTROchemists... take this away from them. They're screwing us!

(There is a bitterness in the room.)

LEN: I see.

(Beat)

BOLTZMANN: *(Quiet)* We didn't have a choice, Len.

(Pause)

LEN: So what are you going to say?

DEWINDT: About?

LEN: The papers. If Thornton brings it up.

STEVENS: You tell us.

LEN: I think—

BOLTZMANN: Just to be clear...he *did* work in hydrogen fusion. What he had not done was work with metals.

(DEWINDT shrugs. The distinction is minor.)

LEN: *(Ignoring the last, continuing)* I think we should prepare for the worst. I think...I mean, in the case of Thornton, I think we should assume he will talk about your betrayal.

DEWINDT: *(Outraged)* Our..!

LEN: What he *considers* your betrayal. And so I think we should address it in our comments. You see, that's the advantage we have. We can preempt whatever he says after by what we say first. And I think Arthur, you should do it. *(On a roll, pressing them)* If Ms Kendle asks about the press conference, the professors should defer it to you. And actually, if it hasn't been asked, you should bring it up. "By the way, there's been a good deal of controversy about the press conference...
(He is cueing DEWINDT, speaking in a deliberate cadence)
...and I just want to say we had no intention of circumventing the process. Quite the contrary..."

(Suddenly the lights change and the men are in the midst of a congressional hearing, DEWINDT picking up LEN's speech without pause. It is the next day.)

DEWINDT: ...we made sure to publish first. The article was already accepted in *The J E A C.*

WOMAN'S VOICE: Tell us about that, please. What is the
J E A C?

*(Quick-paced and smiling, the section that follows is also
rather prickly.)*

DEWINDT: *The Journal of Electroanalytic Chemistry.*

WOMAN'S VOICE: And why was that chosen? Hadn't
you planned to publish in *Nature*?

DEWINDT: We had, yes.

WOMAN'S VOICE: But?

DEWINDT: No "but". We decided to publish in the
J E A C as well.

WOMAN'S VOICE: And is that normal?

DEWINDT: Is what normal?

WOMAN'S VOICE: To publish in two journals at once?
The same paper?

DEWINDT: It is not normal, no. But then you have to
understand. *Nothing* about this process was normal.

BOLTZMANN: *(Interjecting)* If I may?

WOMAN'S VOICE: By all means, please.

BOLTZMANN: *(Smooth, confident)* The *J E A C* is a journal
in which Parker and I had often published. We have
a very strong relationship with the editorial board,
particularly Doug Adkins. We felt, and looking back
now, we may have been mistaken in feeling this way—
but at the time, we felt it was important for us to have
the paper in editorial hands as soon as possible. We
knew we could get it to Doug overnight. And so that's
what we did.

WOMAN'S VOICE: And why did you think that was
important?

BOLTZMANN: *(Beat, thrown)* Well, again, I—

STEVENS: *(Interjecting, edgy)* If I may?

WOMAN'S VOICE: Go ahead.

STEVENS: I think it's important to understand that we did not approach the J E A C. I received a call from Doug Adkins on a separate matter, a totally unrelated matter, and during the course of that conversation I mentioned to him the research we were doing. And he said he was very interested in it. He asked if he could see it. I told him I would have to discuss it with Otto first...but that I would get back to him.

WOMAN'S VOICE: And that's what you did.

STEVENS: Yes.

WOMAN'S VOICE: *(Beat)* I see. *(Then)* So you did not *approach* the J E A C?

STEVENS: We did not, no.

DEWINDT: *(Dovetailing, unctuously)* And as I say, we had no desire to circumvent the process. Unfortunately, this whole...well, you see what we've ended up with here. This whole...episode has been outside the bounds of anything we could have imagined. What we have tried to do, what we have *always* tried to do, is to balance the needs of the media, of the public...with the rigors of science. And frankly, that's been a difficult balance to achieve.

(At this, the lights revert back to the hotel room.)

LEN: Which was brilliant.

BOLTZMANN: Not half so brilliant as what came after.

LEN: What?

STEVENS: You didn't hear?

(The entire group is suddenly very excited, talking quickly.)

LEN: I had to step away.

BOLTZMANN: Parker talked about the cell.

LEN: What cell?

BOLTZMANN: We brought a cell to boil.

LEN: You... *(Agitated)* ...what??

BOLTZMANN: About three months ago...

STEVENS: *(Interjecting)* Four.

BOLTZMANN: ...Parker and I brought a cell to boil.

STEVENS: And Arthur got Jensen to ask about it.

LEN: Who's Jensen?

BOLTZMANN: Our Congressman.

DEWINDT: Must have been right after you stepped out.

STEVENS: Jensen leaned forward, said I wonder if you fellas have a demonstration of some kind, something that could *prove* to us cold fusion.

BOLTZMANN: And Parker said...

STEVENS: As a matter of fact, we do. And I went on to explain it.

LEN: *(Beside himself)* Well, explain it! I don't know about this.

STEVENS: Actually, it's not too different from the meltdown. I went over one day and turned on a cell— and when I came back twenty minutes later, it was boiling.

BOLTZMANN: Which could mean only one thing.

DEWINDT: It had to be nuclear.

LEN: *(Confused)* It couldn't...there—

BOLTZMANN: It couldn't be electrical. We were using the same current.

STEVENS: It couldn't be chemical.

BOLTZMANN: It had to be nuclear.

LEN: *(Excited)* And you told them this!

(BOLTZMANN nods.)

LEN: And what did they say?

STEVENS: Nothing.

BOLTZMANN: For a long moment they didn't say anything. They were just stunned.

DEWINDT: And then the guy at the end, the guy... where was he from?

STEVENS: Nebraska.

DEWINDT: Said how does fifty million sound?

LEN: I don't believe this.

STEVENS: Then the chairman said, well let's not get ahead of ourselves. Though fifty million does sound like a good number.

LEN: *(Practically shouting)* For us? This is fifty million for us?

DEWINDT: I think.

(He looks at the others.)

BOLTZMANN: That's what I think, yes.

LEN: This is unbelievable. You guys are amazing.

DEWINDT: And we left it...how did we leave it?

BOLTZMANN: Well, they're done with us. We're... they want to hear from Len tomorrow. They have questions for him.

DEWINDT: And me.

BOLTZMANN: And you.

STEVENS: But basically, we're in very good shape.

DEWINDT: We're—

LEN: Jesus, from the beginning, and that press conference thing...the publicity...to fifty million! *(He is excited, marveling)* I'm not sure where *my* job comes in.

STEVENS: *(Edgy, almost sharp)* Well, where did you go?

LEN: Pardon?

STEVENS: When you left, where did you go?

LEN: Oh. I was out, I...actually, I was making some calls on the basis of your earlier testimony. Trying to...there's a guy I know from Davos who might be helpful to us. *(Then, suddenly)* In fact, I should call him now. *(Getting up, heading to the door)* I'll be in my room. If you need me... *(Turning back)* ...I'll be in my room.

DEWINDT: Len!

(About to leave, LEN *again turns back—and* DEWINDT *lifts an imaginary glass to him.)*

DEWINDT: Cheers.

LEN: Cheers.

(And with that, LEN *exits. Once he's gone, the other three men look at each other. Clearly all of them are quite pleased.)*

DEWINDT: Nice fellow.

BOLTZMANN: Very nice.

STEVENS: I was just wondering though. Do we need him?

DEWINDT: What do you mean?

STEVENS: Well, I mean...what purpose is he serving?

DEWINDT: Well—

BOLTZMANN: Parker, please. It was because of Len that we answered the way we did. He prepared us magnificently.

DEWINDT: Not to mention the preparation he has done with the committee.

STEVENS: He didn't know who Jensen was!

DEWINDT: Well...still—

BOLTZMANN: What difference does it make? He knows the chairman and the vice-chairman!

DEWINDT: And he has gotten them both to think very highly of us.

STEVENS: Well—

BOLTZMANN: Parker, believe me, there is no one— I can't believe we're saying this—but there is no one we would rather have on our side than Len Spitzer. He is the foremost—am I right about this, Arthur? Help me here—he is the foremost proponent of futurism in our entire country!

STEVENS: Which means what precisely? I mean really, all due respect... *(Irate)* ...what exactly does that mean?

(BOLTZMANN shoots DEWINDT an uneasy look.)

DEWINDT: It means—

STEVENS: I mean...let's be honest here...the guy is a parasite.

BOLTZMANN: Parker!

STEVENS: Otto, he brings nothing to the table. He... I mean, what does he do? He goes looking for technology, for technology breakthroughs, and he hitches his wagon to them. He's the Jesse Jackson of the science world. He adds nothing!

BOLTZMANN: *(To DEWINDT)* Would you... *(He throws up his hands, exasperated.)*

DEWINDT: Parker, Otto is right. He may seem like he's doing nothing—

STEVENS: What is he doing? Really. Explain it to me. What *exactly* is he doing?

(Pause)

DEWINDT: Look, right now he is not...but this *Davos* thing...I mean, this is a man who comes highly recommended. He has represented the largest companies in America. He has represented Apple. He has represented G E. And when they made breakthroughs, when they *had* breakthroughs... he was able to consolidate their positions. He made them a *lot* of money. *(Suddenly, uneasy)* Now, obviously, money...is not—

STEVENS: Oh, don't kid yourself, Arthur. Money is right in the center of this.

DEWINDT: Well, to the extent that it is, I want to make sure our people aren't screwed. I want to make sure the people of our state, of our University, get their fair share. And Len will help us do that.

(A moment passes. DEWINDT is clearly made uncomfortable by his tone.)

DEWINDT: Now, look, let's not talk about this anymore. I mean, hell, we had a great day today! Didn't we have a great day? Otto?

BOLTZMANN: Yes, we did.

DEWINDT: Well, let's celebrate, dammit! Shouldn't we celebrate?

(At this he looks at STEVENS, who looks back at him blankly. Then...)

STEVENS: What the hell. *(And with that, he gets to his feet.)*

DEWINDT: There we go! That's the spirit! And I'll tell you something right now, gentlemen. I'm buying. I don't want to hear any argument. I'm buying!

(With that, he links arms with STEVENS—*he,* STEVENS *and* BOLTZMANN *making their way to the door.)*

DEWINDT: God, what a day, huh? I'll tell you... *(His voice trailing off)* ...

(By now the three men are in the hallway...as the lights fade to black.)

(End Scene Two)

Scene Three

(Later that night. The lights come up on LEN, *who is again on the phone.)*

LEN: *(Excited)* What did you think?

LAURA: It's not good.

LEN: What?

LAURA: What I'm hearing.

(The lights come up then on LAURA.*)*

LEN: *(Sputtering, frustrated)* What...Laura, did you hear what happened today?

LAURA: I did.

LEN: They had a cell boil!

LAURA: Not today they didn't.

LEN: Ten weeks ago!

LAURA: Still. It doesn't prove anything.

LEN: Laura, for Christ's sake—

LAURA: Can I come over?

LEN: What?

LAURA: I need to come over. Can I come over?

(Before he can answer, LAURA *is standing in front of him.)*

LEN: Laura, I—

LAURA: They had no controls.

LEN: They... *(Off-balance, confused)* ...what are you talking about?

LAURA: Do you know what a control is?

LEN: Of course, I—

LAURA: Tell me.

LEN: Laura—

LAURA: It's the guarantee of causality. "It's been conclusively proven that the beating of tom-toms restores the sun after an eclipse." *(As she talks, she throws her coat over a chair, her manner driven, intense, almost angry.)*

LEN: *(Incredulous, lost)* What?

LAURA: Do you believe that tom-toms restore the sun after an eclipse?

LEN: Of course not.

LAURA: *(Snaps)* How do you know that?

LEN: I—

LAURA: And better still, how do you argue with someone, an ancient man say, when he tells you that hundreds of experiments have proven that very fact?

LEN: *(Confused, exasperated)* Laura—

LAURA: It's a fallacy, Len. But because it's never been tested, it's never been disproved. Ancient man believes the beating of tom-toms will restore the sun and so he beats the tom-toms. And the sun, in every instance, is restored. *(By now she is speaking very quickly, almost without pause)* But he never tries not beating the tom-toms and instead taking a bath. Or slaughtering his animals. Or playing his flute. If he had, he would have seen the sun was restored in exactly the same number of instances. In other words, the action of slaughtering the animal or playing the flute or beating the tom-tom had NOTHING to do with restoring the sun. The action was unrelated to the outcome. And that fact is determined by running control experiments. By altering the experimental variable to see if it in fact alters the outcome. But your guys didn't do that. They thought that running a current through deuterated water would result in fusion. But they never tried running it through regular water, through *tap* water. If they had, they might have discovered something entirely different.

LEN: What?

LAURA: That they didn't have fusion, that what they "thought" was fusion, the heat they thought was fusion was actually something else. Because fusion requires neutrons, Len, and hydrogen doesn't have one. Hydrogen, "H", the "H" of H2O, has no neutrons and so if they're getting heat from tap water...it has to be something other than fusion. *(Slight beat)* And so that's the control you would want to run. You would want to see if you got fusion from regular water.

LEN: This is whatsisname.

LAURA: What?

LEN: Your mentor, whatsisname.

LAURA: This is me, Len. This is me asking a regular question.

LEN: On the assumption that...what? I'm a putz?

LAURA: *(Thrown)* What?

LEN: You're making it seem like these concerns of yours, these "issues" you're raising, never occurred to me.

LAURA: Have they?

LEN: Of course they have. This is my job. This is what I'm paid to do. To vet these guys. To *ask* these kind of questions. But look, I need to tell you something. The "t"s are not all crossed on this. The "i"s are not dotted. This thing is moving at breakneck speed...and there are going to be things, this may be one of them...that fall through the cracks. I would hope...that you would know enough about me, about my track record, about the kind of technology I champion...that you would cut these guys a break. *(Beat)* But look, let's get an explanation.

LAURA: What?

LEN: Come with me.

LAURA: Where are we going?

LEN: Let's get...actually, no, you're right. Let's call him.

LAURA: Call?

LEN: Professor Stevens.

LAURA: Prof—

LEN: *(Caught up, impassioned)* Let's bring him down. He'll explain. *(Then, after a moment, fervently)* Let's get an explanation!

(And with that, STEVENS suddenly appears in the doorway—an angry look in his eye.)

STEVENS: *(A beat, then)* Of?

(LAURA steps forward, boldly, almost confrontationally...)

LAURA: Why you didn't run control experiments.

STEVENS: *(Taken aback)* Pardon me?

(He turns to LEN.*)*

LEN: I thought you could explain it.

STEVENS: Len—

LEN: Here, please, come inside.

*(*STEVENS *steps into the room.)*

STEVENS: Len, could I...talk to you?

LAURA: Could you answer me first? *(This last comes aggressively from her.)*

STEVENS: *(Offended)* Pardon?

LAURA: Why you didn't run controls.

STEVENS: *(Beat)* We did.

LAURA: *(Confused)* You—

STEVENS: You're referring to Dallas, I assume.

LAURA: Yes.

STEVENS: *(Then, to* LEN*)* There was a chemistry conference in Dallas. A physicist there, a famous physicist I'm told, asked the same question.

LAURA: And you said to him you didn't. That you had only run the controls recently.

STEVENS: That's right.

LAURA: But now you're telling me something different.

STEVENS: I am, yes.

LAURA: Why?

STEVENS: Because it's the truth. *(Then)* Actually, could... please... *(He looks at* LEN, *cocking his head. Then, to* LAURA*)* ...we'll be right back.

(He then moves away quickly, taking LEN's *elbow.)*

STEVENS: *(Hissing, urgent)* Who is this?

LEN: A friend of mine.

STEVENS: And?

LEN: What do you mean, "and"?

STEVENS: Why am I talking to her?

LEN: She can be helpful.

STEVENS: In what way?

LEN: She's a journalist.

STEVENS: *(Incredulous)* She's a what???

LEN: She's a journalist who is ready to help us. *(This last he says patiently.)* But she has some questions to ask and I think it would be good for us to answer them. *(Slight pause)* Professor, look, she is not asking anything that isn't going to be asked elsewhere. The difference is she may accept your answers where other people might not. Now, come on.

(With that, LEN touches STEVENS's elbow and STEVENS, reluctantly, returns with him.)

STEVENS: I'm sorry, I...what were you asking?

LAURA: About the controls.

STEVENS: Yes.

LAURA: Why would you lie at the conference?

STEVENS: Embarrassment. I didn't want to admit that we conducted the controls but hadn't marked down the results. It seemed easier to say that we had done them recently—clearly there was a reason for them—and we would have the results shortly.

(Beat)

LAURA: *(Dubious)* So you did the controls?

STEVENS: We did, yes.

LAURA: And?

STEVENS: And...what you'd expect. No reaction.

(The two stare at each other.)

STEVENS: *(Then, smugly)* Anything else?

LAURA: When did you do these?

STEVENS: *(Smooth, brisk)* Very early on actually. I'm thinking before the meltdown, but it could have been afterward.

LAURA: After the meltdown?

STEVENS: Af...yes. Just... *(Thinking)* ...in fact—

(Then suddenly, the lights change and STEVENS springs forward, calling, as he does, to the floor up above him. He is in his basement.)

STEVENS: Here. Down the stairs. The basement. Here! *(Then, after a pause, quieter)* This way.

(STEVENS is transfixed, staring at a tabletop. After a moment, having run down the stairs, BOLTZMANN joins him—breathless.)

BOLTZMANN: *(Excited)* What?

STEVENS: You were right.

BOLTZMANN: What?

STEVENS: You were right!

BOLTZMANN: I—

STEVENS: Look!

(Here STEVENS points at the tabletop—and there in front of them is an astonishing sight—a hole four inches deep burned straight through the concrete.)

BOLTZMANN: Where's the cell?

STEVENS: It burned a hole, Otto. It burned a hole right through the table.

BOLTZMANN: It... *(Astonished)* ...what???

(BOLTZMANN rushes to the table, peering into the hole. STEVENS comes up behind him, looking over his shoulder.)

STEVENS: Last night at ten o'clock I sent my son down here. I told him to lower the voltage. That's ALL I told him; and that's ALL he did. And then this morning he came back in to raise it again. *(Beat)* And this is what he found.

(Beat)

BOLTZMANN: *(Hoarsely, whispering)* And he came to get you?

STEVENS: Yes.

(They both continue to stare. In silence.)

BOLTZMANN: What do you think?

STEVENS: *(Quivering, excited)* I'm...asking you.

BOLTZMANN: I think we had ignition. I think...this is it!

STEVENS: Do you?

BOLTZMANN: Absolutely.

STEVENS: But—

BOLTZMANN: Describe what was here yesterday.

STEVENS: What was—

BOLTZMANN: *(Impatient, almost angry)* The experiment. What were the conditions? What did we have? *(His voice is raised a little.)*

STEVENS: Unchanged. A beaker, lithiumdeuteroxide— the palladium, of course, the cube, the—

BOLTZMANN: What size was the cube?

STEVENS: A centimeter.

BOLTZMANN: A full centimeter?

STEVENS: Yes.

BOLTZMANN: *(Turning back)* Well...clearly we can't do that again. *(Beat, staring in)* And this is what's left.

STEVENS: *(In wonder)* What do you think?

(BOLTZMANN *removes a small metal pointer from his pocket. He pokes into the hole.)*

BOLTZMANN: What would you say, three inches?

STEVENS: Four.

BOLTZMANN: And the cube..? Partially vaporized.

STEVENS: I don't...do you see anything?

BOLTZMANN: Some. I think. Do you?

(BOLTZMANN *steps aside so* STEVENS *can see.)*

STEVENS: No, I...don't think so.

(Beat)

BOLTZMANN: And it simply stopped.

STEVENS: As far as we can tell.

BOLTZMANN: And we're alive, so...I don't think there was any radiation.

STEVENS: Not...appreciable.

BOLTZMANN: This is incredible. I mean, my goodness, do you know what this means? Everything I have ever thought might happen is proved by this effect. Coehn was right, Butler, Gurney, I. I, Parker. I was right! *(He turns to him, exultant, his eyes blazing with pride. Then, quieter)* I was right.

STEVENS: The question is how we proceed. I don't want to do this here anymore.

BOLTZMANN: No, I don't think we should.

STEVENS: And if we take this...I mean, we'll have to draw up some safeguards.

BOLTZMANN: Bring in some physics people, some lab people.

STEVENS: But Otto, look, I...I mean, forgive me, but I don't want to lose control with this. I mean, if this is what you think it is...this is HUGE!

BOLTZMANN: Agreed.

STEVENS: And—

BOLTZMANN: But Parker, look...this is something we should not play with. We must, and I emphasize MUST, get support for this! We—

(Suddenly the lights return to LEN *and* LAURA.*)*

LAURA: *(Excited, captivated)* And you knew right then?

STEVENS: *(Also excited)* We...had a sense, yes.

LAURA: And that's when you did the controls?

STEVENS: Actually, no, as I think of it, it was before. *Well* before. You see the thing is, we never expected this to be a paper. We never expected this to come to fruition. This whole thing was an idle curiosity, a LARK... *(Having raised his voice a bit, he now lowers it.)* ...that turned out to pay off enormously.

LAURA: You...don't... *(Truly confused)* ...I don't understand.

STEVENS: In papers where we're serious, where we think we have a...chance of succeeding, we take enormous care. This is generally areas where we've been working for years. Where the new paper is just a small step from the old. And this new step, this baby step...we have every expectation that this new step will bear fruit. That we'll discover what we expect to. And so we prepare for it. We *know* we're going to have a

publishable paper and one of the requirements for a
publishable paper is to report control experiments.
And so we conduct them—jotting down the results,
and have them ready, in our lab books, for publishing.
But in this case, we *didn't* think we had a paper. And so
the idea of jotting down the results would have been
ludicrous. We simply conducted the controls for our
own benefit and then we moved on. And then we
found, much to our surprise, that we *did*, in fact, have
a publishable paper. What we didn't have...were the
controls. *(Beat)* And perhaps we made a mistake in
going ahead without them... *(Slight beat)* ...but
that's...what we did.

(LEN *looks over at* LAURA, *who stares back at* STEVENS.)

LAURA: I see.

LEN: The error...what you're saying is the error was a
function of surprise. You were not expecting success.

STEVENS: We were not, no. In fact, I'd go further than
that. We were shocked...both of us, truly, SHOCKED
when it came to pass.

LEN: And actually, if I can interject, their method...
and you'll forgive me for saying this...but their method
was not normal. Right? They weren't considering these
experiments for publication. They were outside, in the
garage, playing—like a couple of school kids.

LAURA: *(Suddenly, with dawning understanding)* Who
happened to stumble on the discovery of the century.

STEVENS: Exactly.

(Beat)

LAURA: Well, that would explain a lot.

LEN: Laura, it explains *everything*. That's why I wanted
the Professor to come down and talk to you. It explains
everything.

STEVENS: Actually...there is something else that you're probably aware of...that also played a role. There was another man...another—

LAURA: Gilbert Thornton.

STEVENS: Yes. And that...further complicated our process.

(Pause)

LAURA: Well, I have to tell you...there *are*...lots of questions out there. I mean, you guys haven't done yourselves any favors.

STEVENS: I realize that.

LEN: What we're counting on...and again, if I can interject...but what we're counting on...is fairness. That's all. And maybe a little bit of time.

LAURA: Could I...do you mind if I ask you one other thing?

(STEVENS glances over at LEN, clearly at the end of his rope, before turning back to LAURA.)

STEVENS: *(Grudging)* No.

LAURA: There was no raw data in the paper. I mean, correct me if I'm wrong, but isn't a paper, particularly a ground breaking paper, supposed to contain a lot of raw data? Isn't that...I mean, isn't that the way that other labs, other investigators will be able to get your results?

STEVENS: *(Uneasy)* Well...that...

LAURA: But your paper didn't do that. Your paper contained only digested data and that has allowed *nobody* to get your results.

STEVENS: That is not... *(Infuriated)* ...first of all, I reject that! We have had several people get our results. But even...look, there is a simple explanation for what you're describing. It is the difference between physics and chemistry. In chemistry it is perfectly normal to publish a preliminary paper. And that's what we did. We published a *preliminary* paper, we did not publish a final paper. And preliminary papers lack data. That... *(Suddenly outraged)* ...and that brings up another point, by the way. Our news conference! In chemistry, if you look at the journals, you will see that announcements are made all the time. "Such and such a discovery is about to be published." Well, this is allowable as soon as your paper is accepted for publication. As ours was with the *J E A C*. In physics, such an announcement is unheard of. And that is the problem right there. We have been operating under a set of assumptions governing chemists, not physicists. So the fact that we made an announcement, and couple that with the fact that we published a paper missing the data they expected, and our entire enterprise has been called into question in a manner I consider *most* unfair. We will *absolutely* publish a final paper. And I guarantee you it will contain every *bit* of data that's expected. *(Righteously indignant)* In the meantime, I wish that people who had questions for us would come to us directly—rather than going to the media first to smear us.

(Beat)

LAURA: *(Stunned)* I...

(It's clear that STEVENS *has impressed her enormously.)*

LEN: Professor, thank you. Thank you for taking your time with us. *(He leans in, whispering)* It was worth it. I promise you.

*(*STEVENS *shakes* LEN's *hand.)*

STEVENS: Right. *(Then, to* LAURA*)* Good night.

(And with that, he quickly turns out. Once he's gone, LEN *then turns back to* LAURA.*)*

LEN: So?

LAURA: *(Beat)* Explains a lot.

LEN: *(Relieved, confident)* It does, doesn't it.

LAURA: But Len, I have to tell you... *(She turns to him.)* ...these guys are in trouble.

LEN: No kidding.

LAURA: So the question—

LEN: Laura, look, before we...what's *your* stake in this?

LAURA: What do you mean?

LEN: Did you talk to your editor?

LAURA: I did, yes.

LEN: And?

LAURA: And. We're not sure. I mean, he's nervous— as I thought he'd be. And we're not sure where I fit in.

LEN: How...what do you mean?

LAURA: What the story is. For me.

(By now they are next to the chair where LAURA *has left her coat.)*

LEN: The story—

LAURA: Len, we know what the story is for YOU. We're not sure what it is for me.

LEN: The story is the same for everyone, Laura. It's the simple truth.

LAURA: Told in how many installments? Over what period of time? The simple truth and nothing but the simple truth? Or the simple truth from certain angles, and perspectives, given certain understandings?

(Beat)

LEN: The—

LAURA: Len, I won't be your mouthpiece. O K?
I can't be. I will follow this story. I...and I have to vet
everything, by the way, with the science writer, with
Hensley. But I will follow this story. And I will be
scrupulously fair! But I can't tell you how often I'll
publish. And I can't tell you what it is I'll write about.
What I can tell you...is I won't be your flack. I won't
be available to counter every assertion by every source
in every situation that you consider vaguely unfair.
What I will do...well, I've said what I will do. I will
watch this story with interest and objectivity and
detachment. I hope you'll consider that fair.

(Beat)

LEN: O K.

(With that, she reaches for her coat.)

LEN: What are you doing?

LAURA: I should be going.

LEN: I...thought...

LAURA: Leonard. If I'm covering this story...
(She comes near to him.) ...I should be going.

*(With that, she taps him on the lips and starts to turn,
when LEN reaches out for her—taking hold of her hips.)*

LEN: WAIT...a minute. Not even a kiss?

*(The two are now very close—and LAURA is clearly tempted
by this. She debates whether to kiss him. Finally, she shakes
her head.)*

LAURA: Not even a kiss. *(And with that she breaks
away—heading to the door.)*

LAURA: See you. *(Until soon, she's gone. Then...)*

LEN: Damn.

(As the lights slowly fade to black.)

(End Scene Three)

Scene Four

(The next morning. The hotel suite. DEWINDT *sits in a chair alone.)*

DEWINDT: The point is... *(This last he says emphatically. Then, after waiting a minute, he adds, plaintively...)*

DEWINDT: Are you listening to me?

*(*BOLTZMANN *leans out from the bedroom, knotting his tie.)*

BOLTZMANN: We're both listening, Arthur. *(He then disappears again.)*

DEWINDT: *(Calling)* The point is...he's a professional. If he...if this is what he thinks we should do, this is what we should do!

*(*STEVENS *marches out from the bedroom, furious.)*

STEVENS: I don't like being shanghaied like that.

DEWINDT: Oh, now, come on, Parker.

STEVENS: Come on what!

DEWINDT: You were not shanghaied, for God—!

STEVENS: I most certainly was!

BOLTZMANN: *(Off)* You know... *(He strolls out casually from the bedroom.)*

BOLTZMANN: *(Blithely)* I never heard what happened...exactly. I wonder if you could fill me in.

STEVENS: Last night at ten o'clock, after ten o'clock... *(He is furious.)* ...Len brought me down to his hotel room and confronted me with a lady reporter.

BOLTZMANN: Oh?

STEVENS: "Oh." Yes! Asking *very* aggressive questions.

LEN: Which I thought you could handle.

(STEVENS *spins around and sees* LEN, *surprisingly, standing in the doorway.*)

STEVENS: And what if I hadn't!

LEN: You did.

STEVENS: But what if I hadn't!!!

LEN: We'd have gone to Plan B.

STEVENS: Oh, well, that's—

LEN: Fellas, listen to me, I gotta be honest with you. This is a high wire act. This whole thing is a high wire act. We can't keep ourselves insulated. You're gonna have to answer questions, and I think it's better when the questions come from people we know than people we don't.

BOLTZMANN: How well do we know this person?

LEN: Very...well.

DEWINDT: And...I mean, what's going to come of this?

LEN: Who knows? (*Then*) Did you see the paper today?

DEWINDT: The..?

LEN: *The Times. (He tosses it down in front of them.)* It's not entirely flattering. I mean, there's positive stuff in it. But there are also some questions. Some of the same questions our friend was asking. Now my hope is... (*Turning from* STEVENS *to the others*) ...that our friend will also write a story, tomorrow maybe, and answer some of these questions... (*Back to* STEVENS) ...with the answers you gave her. Which again, I think, were very good.

DEWINDT: Makes sense to me.

LEN: Gentlemen... *(He searches.)* ...this is not... *(Again he takes a moment, wanting to phrase it right.)* ...you're not in your lab anymore. You're out in the real world...with an enormous announcement. You can't hide from it.

STEVENS: *(Outraged)* We are not... Please, God, we are not hiding from it! We are... *(Practically sputtering, to* BOLTZMANN*)* Are you listening to this? We are not hiding from it, Leonard. We are appearing before Congress, a committee of Congress, which has asked us back in again! We are meeting the Physics Society! We are seeing the President!

LEN: What is he talking about?

(This last causes LEN *to turn to* DEWINDT, *alarmed.)*

DEWINDT: What?

LEN: They have asked us back in again—what does that mean?

DEWINDT: We got a call. This morning. They want to see us again.

LEN: They...what!

DEWINDT: They want to see you, they're still interested in you. But they also want to see us.

LEN: For what reason?

DEWINDT: They didn't say.

(Suddenly LEN *spins around, facing* LAURA *across the stage.)*

LEN: Do you know about this?

LAURA: No.

LEN: What does it mean?

LAURA: I... *(Worried)* ...I'll have to look into it.

LEN: Is it bad, do you think?

LAURA: I'll have to look into it!

(This last she says sharply, then disappears—forcing LEN *to turn back to the others.)*

DEWINDT: What did she say?

LEN: *(Worried)* She'll have to look into it.

BOLTZMANN: When you asked if it was bad.

LEN: *(Beat)* She said she didn't know. *(Then, immediate)* All right, look, let's...this doesn't have to be bad, right? It could...they might want to rush us the money, right? Isn't that possible?

DEWINDT: That's possible.

BOLTZMANN: We're not ready for it.

DEWINDT: But still, that's...we would be fine. We'd set up an escrow account.

LEN: So that's...I mean, it's at least possible it might not be bad. Right?

(He surveys the room—and the long faces give him his answer.)

LEN: But we should probably be thinking about what to do if it is. *(To* DEWINDT*)* Do you have any ideas?

DEWINDT: I don't, no.

STEVENS: Oh, this is ridiculous! *(Suddenly he stands.)*

LEN: What do you mean?

STEVENS: I mean, I'm tired of this. I'm tired... Look, I don't give a shit about these people. If they want to give us the money, fine. If they DON'T want to give it to us, fine. I'm tired of being grilled like a criminal of some kind. I am not a criminal! I don't want to be grilled!

*(*LEN *and* DEWINDT *look at each other. Then...)*

LEN: Look, this—

(Then suddenly the lights change and LAURA *appears again across the stage.)*

LAURA: It's the physicists.

LEN: The what?

LAURA: They brought in two physicists. They had some questions.

LEN: What kind of questions?

LAURA: Something to do with gamma rays.

LEN: *(Confused)* With...what?

LAURA: With gamma rays. With—

(Again LEN *spins around to the others.)*

LEN: Do you know about this?

BOLTZMANN: About?

LEN: Gamma rays.

STEVENS: Oh, for... *(Again he stands.)*

LEN: Where are you going?

STEVENS: I'm not doing this, Len. I'm not...fuck these people. I'm not doing this! *(And with that, he stomps off.)*

LEN: Parker, don't...

(But before he can finish, STEVENS *has slammed the door to the bathroom—and* LEN *turns to the others.)*

LEN: Would someone please tell me what's going on?

(Silence)

LEN: Otto, would you tell me what's going on?

BOLTZMANN: It's hard to say.

LEN: Guess.

(Beat)

BOLTZMANN: Well, if I had to guess...I'd say Parker's upset.

LEN: Yeah, I got that. About what?

BOLTZMANN: *(Faltering)* About...there are...

DEWINDT: Clearly, this is a stressful time. I think we're all upset.

LEN: About what! Look, I gotta tell you, I'm...I keep feeling like I'm being blindsided here. Like I'm learning things I should already know. *(Suddenly, with force)* Tell me about gamma rays.

(And again LAURA appears.)

LAURA: It's like this...

(But this time instead of disappearing, BOLTZMANN remains in the light, actually his own pool of light, as he and LAURA speaking as one, uninterrupted, their tone both forceful and dynamic, lecture, facing out, as if in a lecture hall.)

BOLTZMANN: It's called "neutron capture on proton."

LAURA: When atoms collide, they produce a neutron.

BOLTZMANN: The neutron is captured by the hydrogen in the water around the cell...

LAURA: ...forming a deuterium atom...

BOLTZMANN: ...which in turn releases a gamma ray at precisely 2.22 million electron volts of energy.

LAURA: It's always precisely this.

BOLTZMANN: Two point two two MeV.

LAURA: What my friend described as the first thing you get in quantum mechanics.

BOLTZMANN: If you get that, in other words...

LAURA: ...if you see a gamma ray coming out at two point two two...

BOLTZMANN: ...you know exactly what's taking place.

LAURA: Fusion.

BOLTZMANN: Another way of saying this...

(And suddenly LAURA *disappears, leaving* LEN *alone with* BOLTZMANN *and* DEWINDT.*)*

BOLTZMANN: *(No longer lecturing, conversational)* ...is the line of the spectrum of two point two two, if you see that line, you know you've got neutron capture on proton. You're generating neutrons.

LEN: And?

BOLTZMANN: Please?

LEN: How...what's the problem?

*(*BOLTZMANN *shifts, clearly uncomfortable.)*

BOLTZMANN: I don't know.

LEN: Otto, please! What—

STEVENS: We didn't have two point two two. We had two point five.

*(*LEN *turns and sees* STEVENS *standing in the doorway. He is furious.)*

LEN: Meaning?

BOLTZMANN: Parker—

STEVENS: Meaning it might not be fusion. If you concentrate purely on this spectrum, it might not be fusion.

*(*LEN *shakes his head, confused.)*

LEN: I don't understand.

STEVENS: I wouldn't think you would. And yet you, like these others, are more than willing to pontificate, aren't you?

DEWINDT: Parker.

STEVENS: No, I'm tired of this. I'm tired...it's bad enough that we have to put up with it out there. Now, we have to put up with it here?

BOLTZMANN: I... *(Then)* ...I think—

STEVENS: Listen to me. I want everyone in this room to listen to me. I am not going to let us be crucified. I am not going to walk into a LION'S DEN and let us be crucified.

LEN: How are you going to stop it?

STEVENS: I'm leaving. I'm getting out of town. I'm—

LEN: *(Cutting him off, coldly)* Could you...I mean, just for my edification...could you, please, explain this to me?

STEVENS: Explain what?

LEN: The discrepancy. Between two point two and two point five.

STEVENS: Two point two two.

LEN: Two point two two.

(Beat)

STEVENS: Otto?

(BOLTZMANN swallows, clearly quite nervous.)

BOLTZMANN: We may not...we may have had an artifact.

LEN: Meaning?

STEVENS: *(Brazen, aggressive)* Meaning we're not certain we got a correct reading. But we had to have it. We had to include it in our paper. And so we adjusted it. *(Suddenly LAURA appears.)*

LEN: What does he mean "adjusted it"?

LAURA: They faked it. They made it up. When they learned that the reading should be two point two two, they changed it.

LEN: How do you know that?

LAURA: That's what whatsisname said, the guy from M I T. He said when he saw their spectrum, he measured it off a television screen while they were doing a C N N interview, it was at two point five. Then when they published it in their paper it was at two point two two. Clearly, someone had spoken to them, told them what it was supposed to be and they moved it. They picked the thing up and they moved it!

LEN: *(Lost)* They...

LAURA: They moved it, Len. They fucking moved it!

LEN: They... *(Then suddenly, turning to the others, accusingly)* ...how do you explain that?

BOLTZMANN: We don't. We...it was bad science.

LEN: *(Suddenly, to* DEWINDT*)* Are you listening to this?

DEWINDT: *(Caught)* I am.

LEN: What do you have to say about it?

DEWINDT: I...well, clearly, I'm not happy. I—

STEVENS: *(Pugnacious)* Arthur, look, do you want us to resign? If you want us to resign, we will.

DEWINDT: No...I...don't want you to resign.

STEVENS: Well then, back us up, goddammit! If you don't want us to resign, back us up.

(Beat)

DEWINDT: I will.

*(*LEN *laughs. it's a laugh of incredulity.)*

LEN: Ok, let's...I'd like to review. The spectrum,
the two point five, was bullshit. Is that right?

STEVENS: The two point two two.

LEN: *(Ignoring him)* Was bullshit.

STEVENS: Yes.

LEN: *(Pressing him)* You just made it up.

BOLTZMANN: We made an adjustment. We...this isn't
uncommon actually. This—

LEN: *(Cutting him off, incredulous)* It isn't uncommon to
MAKE UP DATA?

STEVENS: Leonard, here's the deal. Would you like the
deal? Here's the deal. *(He is furious.)* We *have* the heat.
We *have* neutrons. Not enough, but some. Clearly,
something is happening. Something we cannot explain.

(Suddenly the lights change and LEN *picks up* STEVENS's
*speech, speaking with the same energy, fury, and
self-righteousness—and all in front of Congress!)*

LEN: Now, we can allow ourselves to be sidetracked by
discrepancies in data, or we can focus on the miracle.
We *have* the heat. *(Then)* And there is one other thing.
The thing I am actually here to discuss. We are not
alone in the world. At this moment, right now...
actually, this makes me think of an event that occurred
not two weeks ago. When I first got involved in this,
or shortly thereafter, I wanted to see what was going
on in the world. So I called a friend of mine in Japan.
I asked him if he'd heard of cold fusion, if anyone over
there was doing work on it. I called him at ten o'clock
his time and he called me back two hours later. It was
now past midnight in Japan and he told me that he had
spoken to not one but two different labs there still hard
at work at that very moment. And gentlemen, ladies,
that is not at all unusual. That is the way the Japanese

are. That is the reason that every major advance
we have seen over the last twenty years has been
developed overseas. That is true of microwaves.
That is true of supercomputers. That is true of high
definition T V. We cannot let it be true of cold fusion.
If cold fusion is real—and I realize that's a big if...
(He takes a pause.) ...but if cold fusion is real, it will
result in a multi-TRILLION dollar industry. Do
we want—and this is the question we must ask
ourselves—do we want that industry to be located
in Japan or America? I think for twenty-five million
dollars...which is the cost of continuing our research...
the answer should be America. I hope you do as well.

(Having finished his speech, LEN *then leans back...as the
lights slowly fade to black.)*

(End Scene Four)

END OF ACT ONE

ACT TWO

Scene Five

(Friday morning. The hotel suite. BOLTZMANN *is packing his bag.* LAURA *enters behind him.)*

LAURA: Could I—

BOLTZMANN: Pardon me! *(He spins around, startled.)*

BOLTZMANN: *(Unnerved)* I don't believe we've met.

LAURA: No, we haven't. *(She holds out her hand. Smiling)* I'm Laura Scott.

*(*BOLTZMANN *stares at her hand, debating whether to take it. Finally, he does.)*

BOLTZMANN: Otto Boltzmann.

LAURA: Actually, I've met your partner, Mister Stevens, Doctor Stevens. And I'm a friend of Len Spitzer's.

*(*BOLTZMANN *stares at her unmoving.)*

LAURA: I'm a journalist.

BOLTZMANN: Oh. *(Then, realizing who she is)* Oh, yes.

LAURA: I wonder if I could ask you a couple questions?

BOLTZMANN: *(Nervously)* I don't think so.

LAURA: Please, I...it wouldn't take long.

BOLTZMANN: I'm in a big hurry. I—

LAURA: Please.

(And there is something in the tone of her voice that suddenly stops him.)

LAURA: It would be very helpful.

(He watches her for another moment, then, almost imperceptibly, relents.)

BOLTZMANN: I don't have long.

(With that, he goes back to his bag—and she takes out a note pad. Then, casually, as she takes a seat...)

LAURA: I understand you're leaving.

BOLTZMANN: This afternoon, yes. I...actually, we *were* leaving. Now I understand the plans may have changed.

LAURA: Oh?

BOLTZMANN: Yes, I... *(He laughs.)* ...like everything else this week, it's all up in the air.

LAURA: Is this...are you going to Baltimore?

BOLTZMANN: I really can't talk about it.

(He looks up at her casually.)

LAURA: Can you just tell me that? Is it related to that? Or is it the President? Is it...are you meeting with him?

(And this time his tone is more forceful.)

BOLTZMANN: I really can't talk about it.

LAURA: Can I take that as a denial, or..?

BOLTZMANN: *(Quiet, pleading)* I really can't say.

(LAURA studies him a moment—and decides to go easy.)

LAURA: Well, whatever it is...I'm sure it will be exciting. *(Beat)* So tell me...now that the week is over...what do you think?

BOLTZMANN: Of?

LAURA: Congress. *(Then)* Everything actually. Your discovery, Congress...the other scientists who have testified. The whole thing.

BOLTZMANN: Actually, it's been...hard to sort through. Exciting though. As you say.

LAURA: What's been the most surprising?

BOLTZMANN: In what way?

LAURA: Well, in any way. In... *(She shakes her head.)*

BOLTZMANN: The attention, frankly. I still can't quite believe it.

LAURA: How do you mean?

BOLTZMANN: Well, the whole thing. The—

LAURA: Surely, you can't be surprised. I mean, after...actually, I read the other day that your discovery may be worth over three hundred trillion dollars. Not to mention the collapse of the oil industry, the... *(She laughs.)* Surely you can't be surprised given that.

BOLTZMANN: I guess not. Given that.

LAURA: But you're not used to it.

BOLTZMANN: No.

(She nods.)

LAURA: Listen, I'm a lay person. I'm... I wonder if you could walk me through this.

BOLTZMANN: Walk you—

LAURA: Actually, start at the beginning. Would you mind doing that? Start at the beginning. How did this idea come to you?

BOLTZMANN: Well, actually, that's...I think there's been a bit of a misconception there.

LAURA: How so?

BOLTZMANN: People seem to think...it's not like we had a eureka moment in the lab. We didn't. Or if we did, and in a way we did, that isn't what started us. *(Speaking quickly, excitedly)* I've been working on this problem for more than forty years now. I started in 1948. And what we're on now, the discovery we've made now, is just the logical extension of that. It isn't...people act like we were working on something else, a completely different experiment, and out of that experiment came an anomaly, something completely unexpected, and that's what we're following on. But that isn't true. We *expected* this to occur. We *expected* to discover anomalies in t he way hydrogen is absorbed into palladium. And we did! *(He stops himself, realizing suddenly that he has been speaking in a loud, overheated voice.)* I'm sorry that... *(Trying to calm himself)* ...it's just this has got me rather worked up.

LAURA: I understand. *(Then, after a moment)* Actually, I don't. I wonder...could you take me through this? What happened in 1948?

(BOLTZMANN pauses a moment, just a moment, before answering. When he does, it comes out in a torrent.)

BOLTZMANN: In 1948 I discovered the work of Alfred Coehn. He was working on hydrogen dissolution in a lattice and he showed that hydrogen had a charge, a unit charge. Now, of course I also knew about the work of Lange on the Galvani potential, and the work of Gurney and Butler before the War. Well, you could take these ideas and stick them together and come up with a rather interesting conclusion. The only problem is you would have to employ rather complex instrumentation and I didn't have that. So I put the idea off. I put the idea off until the sixties. At that point, another idea occurred to me, actually two others did. *(By now speaking freely, energetically even)* The first was I started to realize that we had a rather poor understanding of solutions. The second was that hydrogen in a lattice could only be understood as part of a multi-bodied effect. In other words, it wasn't one atom we were talking about. We were talking about a *mass* of hydrogen, entering a *compressed* lattice, with an *enormous* electrical charge. Well, I immediately wanted to start work on these ideas when I realized I couldn't. I was at that time the chairman of my department and I realized it was simply incompatible with my position for me to be doing work that was this...extreme shall we say—so I put it off. I put it off for eleven long years. At that point, I received a telephone call from an old student of mine, a friend actually, Parker Stevens, who asked if I wanted to join him. Actually, he said he had some money and a few ideas and wondered if I might have some as well. I said I did, in fact, and within three months we were working together, hard, side-by-side, in his basement.

LAURA: Were you working continuously?

BOLTZMANN: Off and on actually. I was still returning to England. And cold fusion, by the way, was only one of our experiments. We were running three other investigations as well.

LAURA: *(Excited)* And what was it like? What was... actually before I ask that, something else I've been wondering about. The gamma rays.

BOLTZMANN: *(Nervous)* What about them?

LAURA: Can you talk about them?

BOLTZMANN: What would you like to know?

LAURA: Well, it just seems like there's been a lot of controversy about them. Am I wrong?

BOLTZMANN: That's...actually, I'm not prepared to talk about that.

LAURA: Oh?

BOLTZMANN: There *has* been controversy, confusion actually...and I don't think I'll be able to clear it up here. *(Beat)* So I'd rather not comment.

LAURA: Well, how 'bout this then? How 'bout commenting on Michael Emler?

BOLTZMANN: *(Still more nervous)* What about him?

LAURA: Well, you worked with him, didn't you?

BOLTZMANN: Not...no, I wouldn't say that.

LAURA: What would you say?

BOLTZMANN: *(Squirming)* Actually...you'll have to ask Parker that.

LAURA: Didn't he run your neutron counters? Wasn't it his counters in your lab?

BOLTZMANN: As I say...you'll have to ask Parker.

(BOLTZMANN *is suddenly very nervous.* LAURA *smiles.*)

LAURA: I don't understand.

BOLTZMANN: There are...there are things about the lab... *(Then, almost shouting)* ...I don't know everything!

LAURA: But you know Michael Emler, don't you?

BOLTZMANN: *(Beat)* Yes.

LAURA: And he was in your lab, wasn't he? Your physicist?

(BOLTZMANN *doesn't answer.*)

LAURA: I'll tell you the reason I ask. I spoke to him. And he had some very...odd things to say. Among them that Professor Stevens screamed at him. *Screamed* at him that he was trying to "ruin" the experiment. *(Beat)* Don't you find that odd?

(BOLTZMANN *is clearly uneasy.*)

BOLTZMANN: *(Quiet)* You'll have to talk to Parker.

(Beat)

LAURA: You don't find that amazing?

BOLTZMANN: *(Exploding)* I DON'T... *(Suddenly he stops, trying to calm himself)* ...look...there are many things I don't understand—

LAURA: Tell me about them.

BOLTZMANN: *(Overlapping, upset)* But that doesn't mean...I mean, you read the most damning interpretation into each of these! Parker and Michael had an argument. It happens. It's not... what do you want me to say?

LAURA: Do you know what happened since? Recently, in fact, two weeks ago? Emler received a letter from Stevens' lawyer saying he would sue him. If Emler didn't release data supporting your work... *(Sarcastic)* ...Stevens alleges he is *"hiding"* it...Stevens would *sue* him.

BOLTZMANN: *(Beat, quiet)* I didn't know that.

LAURA: Your partner is playing hardball, Professor.

(Beat)

BOLTZMANN: I think...throughout this episode I think we're all...we're very unsure of ourselves.

LAURA: Not your partner. Not Professor Stevens. He's VERY sure of himself.

BOLTZMANN: Look—

LAURA: And the question I have, the real question for me...is why are you going along with him?

(Pause)

BOLTZMANN: *(Suddenly honest)* I don't have a choice.

LAURA: What do you mean?

BOLTZMANN: The work we're doing... *(He swallows, thinking of what to say)* ...we have made genuine... *(Again he swallows.)* ...there are many things about the way we have handled this episode that I regret. *(Then)* But what's done is done. We can't go back. All we can do...is make sure the work we do from here on...is absolutely first rate.

(LAURA regards him for a short moment.)

LAURA: The first page of your paper contains a spectrum. A partial spectrum actually. Tell me how you arrived at it.

(Pause)

BOLTZMANN: *(Again nervous)* I was given the data by Parker. I had been in England and when I returned I was given the data by Parker. I simply plotted the graph.

LAURA: And when it matched what you expected, when it showed two point two two, you simply accepted it.

BOLTZMANN: Yes.

(Pause)

LAURA: And what have you learned since?

(BOLTZMANN looks at her with great pain in his eyes. Then, finally...)

BOLTZMANN: I've learned... *(Then, after a beat)* ...look, I don't—

LAURA: *(Harsh)* What have you learned, Professor?

(Beat)

BOLTZMANN: I've learned the numbers were cooked.

LAURA: *(Pressing)* He made them up.

BOLTZMANN: Yes.

(Beat)

LAURA: And—

(But before she can continue, STEVENS suddenly flies through the door.)

STEVENS: They found it! *(Then, immediately)* What are you doing here?

LAURA: I—

STEVENS: Ah, never mind. It doesn't matter. *(To BOLTZMANN)* Otto, they found it!

BOLTZMANN: They—

STEVENS: At Texas A & M. They found it. They found the tritium.

BOLTZMANN: They're ready to say that?

STEVENS: They're announcing this afternoon.

LAURA: Which means what...exactly?

STEVENS: Which means, my dear, that you can take that story you're writing and tear it up. We've been vindicated.

LAURA: *(Turning, to BOLTZMANN, confused)* How..?

BOLTZMANN: *(Dazed)* Tritium means fusion. To have tritium, you have to have fusion.

(DEWINDT is now standing in the doorway.)

DEWINDT: Isn't that wonderful?

BOLTZMANN: *(Amazed)* Wonderful.

LAURA: Convenient timing.

STEVENS: *(Sharp)* What do you mean?

LAURA: Don't you think?

STEVENS: What are you suggesting?

LAURA: That they should find what you need this week.

STEVENS: What about it?

LAURA: I'm suspicious.

STEVENS: *(Getting hot)* Are you now?

LAURA: I am, yes.

STEVENS: On what basis? Other than the fact that it ruins your story, that all your preconceived notions go flying out the window, on what basis are you suspicious? *(He is now furious.)*

LAURA: I—

STEVENS: Here, I'll tell you what. Before you go making an enormous fool of yourself, why don't you do us all a big favor and find out what you're talking about?

LAURA: I—

STEVENS: Unless of course you don't CARE what you're talking about and only want to prove your point. In that case, of course, you WOULDN'T want to talk to these people. You wouldn't want to learn what you were saying. You would want to go on promoting the same ignorance, the same drivel as you've been doing all along!

LAURA: Rather like you.

STEVENS: *(Beat)* What did you say?

LAURA: Isn't that what you've done?

STEVENS: In what... *(Suddenly, thinking better of the conversation)* ...you know, I don't have to do this. I don't *want* to do this. I'd like you to leave us.

LAURA: I'm not finished yet.

STEVENS: I think you are.

LAURA: *(In a panic, to* BOLTZMANN*)* Professor.

STEVENS: I said, I think you are!

*(*LAURA *turns to* STEVENS.*)*

LAURA: He told me what you did. He told me about the spectrum.

STEVENS: Whatever he told you... *(His teeth clenched, seething)* ...the fact is that we have tritium...and we have heat...and those two things ...mean that we have fusion. *(Beat)* So you, my dear, can kiss my ass.

*(*DEWINDT *comes over to* LAURA*'s side.)*

DEWINDT: Miss. Please.

LAURA: *(To* BOLTZMANN*)* I want to keep on with this. Ask Len for my number.

(And with that, she exits. Once she's gone, STEVENS *immediately turns on* BOLTZMANN.*)*

STEVENS: What is she talking about?

BOLTZMANN: Nothing...I—

STEVENS: Did you tell her about the spectrum?

(Beat)

BOLTZMANN: I did, yes.

DEWINDT: Why?

BOLTZMANN: *(Beat)* I don't know.

(Pause)

DEWINDT: Well, look, Parker, as you say, it doesn't matter. It's—

STEVENS: Arthur! *(Beat)* What did you say exactly?

BOLTZMANN: I just...I said I didn't trust the numbers.

STEVENS: Did you tell her I gave them to you?

BOLTZMANN: Yes.

DEWINDT: Parker—

STEVENS: Arthur, shut up! *(To* BOLTZMANN*)* Why?

BOLTZMANN: I just...

STEVENS: *(Harsh)* Do you want to fuck this up?

BOLTZMANN: No.

STEVENS: Well then, you didn't say that. When she calls back for follow-up, when the story is printed, you didn't say that! Do you understand?!?

*(*BOLTZMANN *and* STEVENS *stare at each other.* STEVENS*is furious.)*

DEWINDT: Look, what's important is the confirmation, isn't it? Isn't that what's important? The tritium?

STEVENS: There are many things important, Arthur. And one of them is my credibility. And we don't need it sabotaged by an old man losing his nerve. *(He stares at* BOLTZMANN.*)* Otto, tell me something. Do you want to go home? Do you want to skip the meeting in Baltimore? Skip the meeting with the President? What do you want to do?

(Pause)

BOLTZMANN: I...

DEWINDT: Don't be ridiculous. We just got confirmation!

*(*STEVENS *continues to stare at* BOLTZMANN. *He shrugs.)*

STEVENS: Go home?

BOLTZMANN: No.

(Beat)

STEVENS: Well then buck the fuck up.

(Suddenly LEN *appears in the doorway.)*

LEN: What's going on?

(There is a silence. Then DEWINDT *forces himself to brighten.)*

DEWINDT: We got confirmation! Parker heard from the people at A & M. We got confirmation!

LEN: Is that true?

*(*STEVENS *breaks off his stare with* BOLTZMANN.*)*

STEVENS: Yeah.

LEN: Well, that's fabulous.

STEVENS: It is, yeah.

(Beat)

LEN: So why do I feel like someone just died?

STEVENS: Well, for one thing, we had an interesting little run-in with your little friend.

LEN: My—

STEVENS: Your little reporter friend? *(Beat)* She found Otto alone here. And the two had a chat.

LEN: *(Nervous)* And?

STEVENS: And? Otto?

DEWINDT: Parker, it doesn't matter. It doesn't...the important thing is confirmation. We got confirmation. We can take that to the President. We can take that to Baltimore. We got confirmation!

*(*STEVENS *turns from* BOLTZMANN *to* LEN. *A moment passes.)*

STEVENS: We're going to have to do something about her.

LEN: What do you suggest?

STEVENS: I don't know. But I don't want to talk to her again. And I don't want her talking to Otto again. Do you understand?

LEN: I understand.

STEVENS: *(Annoyed)* I...you know, Len, if you don't feel comfortable with us, you don't have to stay.

LEN: I feel comfortable.

STEVENS: Well, you make sure, and I'm not joking about this...you make sure I don't see her again.

DEWINDT: Actually...that brings up—

STEVENS: Arthur! *(To* LEN*)* Are we clear?

LEN: We're clear.

(Beat)

DEWINDT: That brings up this afternoon. What ARE we doing?

*(*DEWINDT *looks to* STEVENS *who in turn looks at* LEN*.)*

LEN: The committee is happy. We should keep them that way.

STEVENS: Meaning what?

LEN: Meaning we should do what we said we would. We said we were going to Baltimore, we implied we were meeting the President. We should do those things and head home in triumph. And the money will follow.

BOLTZMANN: Except...

STEVENS: *(Beat, sharp)* Except what?

BOLTZMANN: I have a bad feeling.

DEWINDT: About?

BOLTZMANN: Baltimore. I don't think it will go well.

LEN: Why not?

BOLTZMANN: They're physicists. They'll have questions.

DEWINDT: And we'll have answers! Tritium!

(Beat)

BOLTZMANN: I don't think it will go well.

(Beat)

STEVENS: *(To* LEN*)* What happens if we skip Baltimore?

LEN: It will raise questions. "Why did they skip?"

(Pause)

STEVENS: O K, look, I think we should do it. We'll go to Baltimore, we'll see the President. When are we seeing him?

DEWINDT: The day after tomorrow. In the morning.

(STEVENS *nods.)*

STEVENS: *(Then)* And then we'll head home. And we'll have done everything we needed to, right?

(To this he gets a nod from LEN *and a nod from* DEWINDT. *From* BOLTZMANN, *he gets nothing.)*

STEVENS: Otto, look—

BOLTZMANN: It won't be like Congress. The questions will be harsh. They'll be informed. It won't be like Congress.

(STEVENS *is furious.)*

STEVENS: It'll be fine. As long...and this is important... as long as we're intelligent. And we answer the questions that are asked. And we don't volunteer... *(Getting hotter)* ...unnecessarily...meaningless, misLEADING information that can only CONFUSE!... *(Long beat)* ...we'll be fine.

(There is a long silence.)

STEVENS: Let's meet back at three and catch the train.

(The others look at him and nod.)

STEVENS: See you then.

(And with that, STEVENS exits—as the other three stay behind...and the lights very slowly fade to black.)

(End Scene Five)

Scene Six

(An hour later. LEN's room. LAURA races in on LEN's heels. She is furious. He is packing.)

LAURA: You're joking, right?

LEN: Laura, look, I—

LAURA: He admitted it to me!

LEN: You misunderstood.

LAURA: He said it to my face, Len!

LEN: Look, I'm not saying—

LAURA: Len, why are you doing this?

(LEN spins around, annoyed.)

LEN: Doing what?

LAURA: Sticking with them. I would expect you to be fifty miles from this by now.

(She is now standing in front of him.)

LEN: Laura, for God's sake, they found the tritium!

LAURA: Bullshit.

LEN: What are you talking about?

LAURA: Do you know who "they" is, Len?

LEN: What?

LAURA: "They." The "they" that found the tritium. Do you know who "they" is?

LEN: Who?

LAURA: His teacher. This is Boltzmann's teacher. This isn't an independent guy. This... *(Beside herself)* ...this is another electrochemist!

LEN: So WHAT? He—

LAURA: So how come the greatest people in the field, the scientists at M I T, at Caltech, at Harwell, how come the people at our national labs can't find this tritium... but Boltzmann's mentor; his teacher; his lab buddy... *(Each of these last is said scathingly)* ...CAN?

LEN: *(Thrown)* Because...obviously...

LAURA: Because they're seeing what they want to see.

(LAURA quickly grabs for a chair, placing it down in front of him.)

LEN: Look, I got a half hour. I gotta catch a train.

LAURA: It's called pathological science. *(Beat, she watches him.)* Are you listening to me? It's the opposite of the scientific method. They didn't assemble the known facts and then create a theory. They created a theory and then picked out the acceptable facts.

LEN: That's nonsense.

LAURA: Your guys have fallen into a trap, Len. They want so much to prove their contention that they discount all evidence that DISproves it.

LEN: What do you base this on?

LAURA: Have you ever heard them say something negative about their work? Have you ever heard them say something that would tend to cast doubts about their results?

LEN: Of course!

LAURA: I'm not talking about admissions they were forced to make. I'm talking about volunteering information that reveals self-doubt.

LEN: Laura—

LAURA: You haven't, Len. I guarantee you, you haven't!

LEN: Because they're trying to PROVE something, Laura! They're not trying to DISPROVE it. *(By now he is equally furious—spitting mad.)* Of course, they have a theory, a hypothesis. What's wrong with that???

LAURA: NOTHING! So long as they are objective about their research! So long as when a fact comes in that they *didn't* expect, that *doesn't* confirm their finding, that they give it sufficient weight. That they don't ignore it. But your guys didn't do that. When the spectrum didn't match their expectations, they moved it. When there should have been a billion neutrons and there weren't, they said they had found a new branch. And that brings up another thing by the way. A definitive test. Ask them about helium. When deuterated water absorbs into palladium, assuming it IS fusion, it should fuse a certain percentage of time into helium. Ask them about that. Ask them if they're willing to have their palladium tested.

(Slight beat)

LAURA: Will you do that?

(Beat)

LEN: I might. If you're willing to do something for me.

LAURA: What's that?

LEN: Drop this. Move away.

(Beat)

LAURA: Say what!

LEN: I don't expect the paper to drop it. But let Hensley take over. You move away.

LAURA: Why?

LEN: I don't think you're objective about this.

LAURA: Len—

LEN: The same thing you're accusing them of, I think is true of you. You're not objective about this.

LAURA: You're joking.

LEN: Laura, we got proof. We got incontrovertible proof. But instead of responding with interest, with openness, you immediately begin to cast doubt. You immediately become suspicious. I don't think that's fair.

(LAURA's eyes narrow, now even more suspicious than before.)

LAURA: Were you told to do this?

LEN: What?

LAURA: Were you told to keep me off the story?

LEN: No.

(Short beat)

LEN: I was told to keep you away from them. But I was not told to keep you off the story. That's my idea.

(A pause. LAURA steadies herself. Her fury becomes cold.)

LAURA: Let's say, just for the sake of discussion, that I'm right. That this proof you speak of, this tritium, is bogus. Then what?

LEN: Then...I don't know.

LAURA: How long will you stay with them?

LEN: For...Laura, look, we don't share the same premise.

LAURA: Which is?

LEN: That they're fraudulent. I don't think they are.

LAURA: I don't THINK they're fraudulent. I don't... *(Frustrated)* ...I don't think they are. I think they're blinded. I... *(Suddenly, trying another tack)* A scientist studies the moon. He thinks that it's made of green cheese. But he doesn't look through the telescope to SEE what it's made of. Or if he does, he discounts what he sees; there's obviously something wrong with the lens. And then one day he passes a puddle of water and in that puddle the moon appears green—and THAT'S the fact he holds on to. *(Beat)* Do you see? There's a selectivity. There's a...well, the word pathological. There's a pathological need to steer the investigation to a specific conclusion. The information that CONFIRMS that conclusion is held onto. The information that contests it is dismissed. And that's what these guys have done. They haven't consciously set out to defraud the whole world. They have subconsciously, unKNOWingly, quite innocently, perhaps... promulgated a myth.

(Beat)

LEN: I don't believe that.

LAURA: *(Frustrated)* Based on WHAT? What—

LEN: Laura, these guys, Boltzmann in particular, are *decorated,* hugely successful scientists.

LAURA: Not Stevens. Stevens didn't graduate from college.

LEN: That—

LAURA: Did you know that? The first time he was in college, Len, he didn't graduate.

LEN: He—

LAURA: He went home, into his family business, his family is in textiles...he went home into his family business and then ten years *later* he joined Boltzmann in England.

LEN: At which point he DID graduate. Though. Didn't he? *(He is now furious.)* In fact, he got his Phd.

LAURA: Yeah, but—

LEN: Laura, look, I'm not gonna do this. I mean, fine, Stevens is undistinguished. But that doesn't explain Otto Boltzmann. I mean, Christ—Otto Boltzmann! When did Otto Boltzmann go from being a FELLOW of the Royal SOCIETY...to being a sociopath who can't tell a fact from a myth?

LAURA: *(Beat, certain)* I don't know.

(LEN stares at her.)

LEN: *(Beat, shaken)* Well, he didn't. *(Beat)* I don't believe he did.

(Beat)

LAURA: So you're going to...what, stay with them to the end?

LEN: Till...yes. *(Then, after a moment)* Yes.

LAURA: I see. *(At this, she watches him, nodding her head. Then...)* I pour a drink?

LEN: What?

LAURA: A drink? Can—

LEN: Laura, look—

LAURA: Keep packing. *(Beat, she gestures.)* Keep packing.

(And after a moment, reluctantly, LEN turns back to his suitcase.)

LAURA: I pour you one?

LEN: No! *(Then)* Thank you.

(LAURA *then heads to the dresser, taking hold of the bottle and glass that are waiting there. Then, as she pours...*)

LAURA: So how do you explain all this? When you're asked. I mean, I'm not the only one...nosing around about this.

LEN: You're the most persistent.

(She waits for him to continue.)

LAURA: *(Then, half-turning)* And? What do you say?

LEN: I say the Wright brothers...the WRIGHT BROTHERS, Laura...worked for YEARS...to perfect their aeroplane. And they didn't perfect it in stages. Or the stages, if they existed, weren't visible to most. And do you know what *The Times, The NEW YORK Times,* said the night before they flew? That they were hucksters. That they would never fly. That the public should not be taken in. *(Beat)* I say something like that.

(She smiles—before crossing back.)

LAURA: It's a good answer.

LEN: Thanks.

(Beat)

LAURA: But—

(Suddenly STEVENS appears, facing out.)

STEVENS: *(Sharp, accusing)* Where are you?

LEN: *(Startled)* What?

STEVENS: Where ARE you?

LEN: In my room. *(Confused)* You're calling me in my room.

STEVENS: Have you heard?

LEN: About?

STEVENS: The physicists.

LEN: What about them?

(DEWINDT *suddenly appears.*)

DEWINDT: They're saying we got it wrong.

LEN: They're... *(Then)* ...what?

STEVENS: The heat. *(He is clearly upset. His voice is quavering.)* They're saying we got the heat wrong.

(Beat)

DEWINDT: They're waiting for us in Baltimore. They're...that's what they're going to say.

(Beat)

LEN: So what does that mean?

STEVENS: I don't want to go.

DEWINDT: *(Plaintive, pleading)* Len, we have to.

STEVENS: Arthur, I don't want to get crucified!

DEWINDT: Len...help me with this.

(Beat)

LEN: I don't know what to say.

STEVENS: Len...if the heat's wrong... *(Beat)* ...if... *(Panicking)* ...we don't have anything.

(Beat)

LEN: Is the heat wrong?

(Longer beat.)

STEVENS: I don't know.

DEWINDT: Well, of course, it's not wrong. How *could* it be wrong?

(Beat)

LEN: How could it be wrong?

STEVENS: They're saying we didn't stir it properly. That without stirring it properly, the... *(He stops for a moment)* ...that it could be hotter in one place than another.

LEN: And? Is that true?

STEVENS: I don't... *(About to say "think so", he stops himself. He gives up.)* ...I don't know.

(Pause)

LEN: What does Otto say?

STEVENS: We haven't told him.

LEN: Why not?

STEVENS: We...

DEWINDT: We wanted to talk to you first.

(Pause)

LEN: O K, look, go up to Otto's room.

DEWINDT: Len—

LEN: Just...go up to his room. I'll join you there.

(At this, the lights go out on DEWINDT and STEVENS, as LEN turns back to LAURA.)

LEN: You'll have to leave.

LAURA: What is it?

LEN: *(Sharp)* You'll have to leave! *(He is clearly unnerved.)*

LAURA: Is it Baltimore?

(LEN simply stares at her.)

LAURA: What is it?

(Beat)

LEN: *(Finally)* Everything.

LAURA: Something about the heat?

LEN: There's... *(Then, after a beat, resigned)* ...yeah.

LAURA: What?

LEN: I don't know. I... *(He shakes his head, fatigued)* I don't know.

LAURA: Len, listen to me, I'm telling you this as a friend. Get out of here. Get out of this. Don't... *(She is starting to panic)* ...don't do anymore.

(LEN looks at her.)

LEN: Laura, if I could get out I would. I can't get out.

LAURA: Of course you can.

LEN: *(Loud, harsh)* No, Laura, I can't! I've committed to these people and I've...I've committed to these people! I can't get out. *(Beat)* But hey...you can make this hard for me or easy for me. Whatsay you make it easy for me? Huh?

(LAURA looks at him for a long moment.)

LAURA: O K, Len. *(Beat)* O K.

(And with that, LAURA crosses to the dresser and sets down her drink. She then moves to the door and stops in front of LEN. They stare at each other for a brief moment. Then...)

LAURA: Good luck.

(And with that she exits...as the lights, once again, fade to black.)

(End Scene Six)

Scene Seven

(Later that afternoon. The hotel suite. STEVENS, LEN and DEWINDT are standing around the room. BOLTZMANN is seated. The air is tense. BOLTZMANN has been speaking for some time).

BOLTZMANN: Which is why I want to talk to her.

STEVENS: *(Short)* You talk to her and I go home.

BOLTZMANN: Go.

(STEVENS is surprised by the sharpness of BOLTZMANN's replay—and stung.)

STEVENS: Otto—

BOLTZMANN: *(Suddenly hot, edgy)* Parker, how long are we going to continue this? How long are we going to continue pretending we have answers when we don't?

(Beat)

STEVENS: *(Shaken)* I—

BOLTZMANN: I am not saying we are wrong. We may not be wrong. But we have made errors, that is certain. And we must be forthright on that point.

DEWINDT: To what end? What... *(Clearly worried)* ...what exactly are you prepared to say?

BOLTZMANN: I'll tell you what I will not say. I will not say we were wrong about the heat. Because we were not. The idea that we did not mix the solutions is absurd. There is no—and I say this with the benefit of forty years research—there is no better method of mixing than gas evolution. To think otherwise is ridiculous.

(Beat)

STEVENS: Still—

BOLTZMANN: *(Exasperated)* Still *what*, Parker?

STEVENS: *(Also hot)* I don't see what we get by talking to Ms Scott.

BOLTZMANN: Credibility. She has written articles which more than most seem fair. She has taken us to task, but only, and this is important, ONLY when we deserved it. I think if we speak candidly with her she will be fair.

(Slight beat)

DEWINDT: *(Uneasy)* And? Say what?

BOLTZMANN: That we made mistakes. But that we have found something—and again, this is *important...* *(This last with raised voice)* ...that has yet to be explained.

LEN: She's already said that.

BOLTZMANN: At this point—it's worth saying again.

STEVENS: I'll tell you what I think. I think every time we talk to her we bury ourselves. I think—and I apologize Len for saying this, but it's the way I feel—I think she is out to get us. I think from the outset she has—and maybe it's because she is not a science writer and she felt she had to be overly critical—but she has been determined to discredit us. I think we gain nothing by going to her.

BOLTZMANN: *(Aggressive)* So what do you suggest?

STEVENS: I think we go home.

BOLTZMANN: And do what?

STEVENS: Continue our research.

BOLTZMANN: With what money? *(Bluntly)* Huh? Where is the funding coming from? Do you think Arthur will support us?

STEVENS: Do... *(Turning to DEWINDT)* ...yes!

BOLTZMANN: Arthur?

(DEWINDT looks away, uneasy.)

DEWINDT: I...

LEN: That's not fair.

BOLTZMANN: And I'm not talking about now, either. I'm talking about four months from now, six months. Ten. When we're still hunkered down, when we're still not answering questions. Do you think Arthur will support us *then*?

(*Again* STEVENS *looks at* DEWINDT.)

BOLTZMANN: And Arthur, I'm not casting aspersions. I think you're a fine man. I... I'm just talking about the pressure you're bound to be under. From the academic senate. From... I'm just being realistic. We *have* to answer these questions.

(*A moment passes.*)

LEN: So what do you suggest?

BOLTZMANN: I want to talk to your friend. And then I want to go to Los Angeles.

DEWINDT: Los Angeles??

LEN: What's in Los Angeles?

BOLTZMANN: The Electrochemistry conference. Starting on Monday. We'll get a good reception.

STEVENS: How do you know that?

BOLTZMANN: I've talked to our friends.

STEVENS: Which friends?

BOLTZMANN: Which ones do you think?

(*Beat*)

LEN: And? What have they said?

BOLTZMANN: They're not out to get us. The conference isn't being set up, as the conference in Baltimore so obviously is, to play "gotcha". These are people, and granted they're electrochemists they're not physicists, but these are people who are hoping that cold fusion is real. They're hoping that we have stumbled on something that they, that everyone actually, but that they especially, can get to work on. And I think it's a perfect environment for us to answer these questions. To field them and to answer them.

(*Suddenly the hotel disappears, and* LAURA *and* LEN *appear in two pools of light.*)

LAURA: Except for one thing. They won't be asked.

LEN: What do you mean?

LAURA: They're only accepting positive papers. They're not accepting—and Hensley had never heard of this before—but they're not accepting papers with a critique.

LEN: (*Floundering*) Well—

LAURA: Len, you don't get to pick your enemies! If you want to stop the fighting, you have to go to where the bullets are. And the bullets aren't in Los Angeles.

LEN: Well, they're not going to Baltimore, so I don't know what to tell you.

(*Slight beat*)

LAURA: Do you know who Lou Nathan is?

LEN: Who?

LAURA: He's from Caltech. He spoke here tonight. I watched him.

LEN: And?

LAURA: And it's easy to see why you're not in Baltimore.

LEN: Why? What did he say?

LAURA: No neutrons, no gamma rays, no tritium, no heat. Oh, and no helium either. And do you know what happened after he spoke? Two thousand physicists rose, as one, and gave him a standing ovation.

LEN: And you expect us to go there?

LAURA: But then the most amazing thing. And Len, I have to tell you, this is never, *never* done in a science conference; I asked Hensley about this. Do you know what happened *after* he spoke? When he was talking to the press? He called your guys, and I quote, "incompetent and delusional." Actually he said "possibly" delusional.

LEN: He *said* that?

LAURA: Those precise words. And then he explained why. It seems the third column—do you know in your paper the three columns?—well it seems the third column, the ENTIRE third column...is ENTIRELY made up. There has never, and he was categorical about this, NEVER been an experiment run that gave out those kind of numbers. And do you know why? *(She waits a moment for an answer.)* Because to do so would have contradicted the Third Law of Thermodynamics! *All* the laws actually, but the Third Law in particular, and even your guys, Len...even *your* guys...don't have the nerve, the BALLS to do that.

(She waits again for him to respond.)

LEN: *(Quiet, beseeching)* Laura, he wants to talk to you. That's the bottom line.

LAURA: What does he want to say?

LEN: He thinks you'll give him a fair hearing.

LAURA: Does... *(Then)* ...yeah, sure, I'll talk to him. But Len... *(Then, after a pause)* ...never mind.

LEN: What?

(Beat)

LAURA: Look, they're done. It doesn't matter what I write. They're done.

LEN: Just talk to him.

(As he says this, the lights return to the hotel room where BOLTZMANN *is now standing alone.* LEN *gestures for them to sit down.)*

LEN: So...let's—

BOLTZMANN: Leave us, for a minute, will you?

(LEN reacts in surprise, pulling back.)

LEN: Well, actually—

BOLTZMANN: We'll be all right. And there's something I'd like to say to Miss Scott alone.

(LEN looks from one to the other. He is clearly uneasy.)

LEN: *(Finally)* All right. *(Then)* I'll be downstairs.

(And with that, he exits. Once he's gone, a long moment passes before BOLTZMANN *finally speaks.)*

BOLTZMANN: If you had to say, now, if you had to choose...a word to describe us...what would it be?

LAURA: I... *(Now she is uneasy.)* I'm not sure I could.

BOLTZMANN: Try.

(Pause)

LAURA: I think...rather than have me venture opinions... it would be better if I acquired facts. I'd feel more comfortable doing that.

BOLTZMANN: Do you think we're charlatans?

LAURA: Again, I'm—

BOLTZMANN: I won't talk to you unless you're honest with me. Be honest with me! *(This last is said loudly.)*

LAURA: Professor, I...this is all new to me. I'm not—

BOLTZMANN: Len told me about Baltimore. About what you said.

LAURA: I merely...I reported what Lou Nathan said.

BOLTZMANN: That we were delusional.

LAURA: Yes...that—

BOLTZMANN: And you believe that?

LAURA: *(Uncomfortable)* I don't know, I—

BOLTZMANN: And yet you feel comfortable reporting it.

LAURA: The man who made that statement...is an extremely respected—

BOLTZMANN: Extremely respected?

LAURA: *(Overlapping, defensive)* ...member of that community, yes.

BOLTZMANN: A member of the Royal Society?

LAURA: If he were British, a member of the Royal Society, yes, very likely.

BOLTZMANN: *(Hot)* And just what does that afford him, such exalted status? Certainly not respect.

LAURA: Professor Boltzmann—

BOLTZMANN: *(Cutting her off)* That's all. We don't have to belabor the point.

(Beat)

LAURA: I wonder if you could tell me what you wanted to discuss.

(Pause)

BOLTZMANN: Why I did what I did. Why I continue to do it.

LAURA: Why is that?

BOLTZMANN: Do you have any idea? *(Beat)* What do you think?

(Pause)

LAURA: I think you made a mistake.

(She waits for a response—then...)

LAURA: I think you saw something, or thought you did, and you got very excited. I think you'd confirmed what you'd long suspected. You had a theory, a pet theory, and here was the evidence to support it. And you called out. You called out in excitement. And that's where you made your mistake. *(A brief pause)* Because instead of having someone there who could calm you, who could reason with you, who could show you where you'd made your mistake, you had Professor Stevens, a man who had no interest in pulling you back. Quite the contrary, in fact. *(By now, on a roll)* He wanted you to go forward. He wanted you to continue with a process that for him had no bounds. Because if you were excited, he was beside himself. He was convinced you were on the road to the Nobel, a prize he had never before DREAMED for himself. And so he pushed you. He pushed you continuously. He pushed you to make claims and stake out positions that you had no way of supporting. And so you counseled restraint. You... But every time you did so, he pushed even harder. He belittled you. He demanded that you buck up, have courage. Until one day you found yourself boxed in. *(At this, she slows.)* By this time, you'd made claims in writing, in print, that you couldn't possibly walk away from. And so you had to stick to them. Even if it meant being uncovered, unmasked... *(Really taking her time now)* ...having your entire career called into question. Everything that has puzzled everyone that has ever known you...or written about you...over the last forty years.

(She then pauses, allowing what she has said to settle in. Then...)

LAURA: That's why I think you did it. Why you continue to do it...I don't know.

(Pause)

BOLTZMANN: *(Softly)* Because of my pet theory.
*(He is deeply moved; his voice, when he continues,
a mixture of sadness and grim humor.)*

BOLTZMANN: And because...do you know how old
I was when I published my first book? Twenty-six.
When I won my first prize? The Cederling Medal?
Thirty-one. And in the ten years after that, well,
I was tenured, I became chairman of my department,
but I also won every prize there was to win.
In chemistry, that is. I won the Cederling again.
I won citation after citation. I was elected to the
Royal Society by the time I was forty-five. *(Beat)* Which
was also around the time I published my last book.

(Longer pause)

BOLTZMANN: And since then, since that last book...I
have waited for another moment, another achievement,
another inspiration to strike me. *(Beat)* And it never did.
At first I marked it down to bad luck. Fatigue. Going
through a dry patch. And then it occurred to me. I was
done. As year bled into year, and decade into decade,
I realized I would never again have the pleasure I had
so loved as a young man. I would never again...make
a discovery that everyone, the world over, would
recognize as brilliant. *(Long pause)* Until this. Until the
moment in Parker's kitchen, when I again outlined an
idea, and again saw a look come onto another man's
face. A look that said I was brilliant. That I had once
again thought of something—something important—
that no one else had imagined. And I can't tell you how
that made me feel.

(Pause)

BOLTZMANN: Old age does terrible things to us. But one
of the worst things it does...is to take away our pride.
And, paradoxically, our humility as well. The result is

we do stupid, careless things...and can't seem to stop ourselves.

(Slight beat)

LAURA: Why?

(Beat)

BOLTZMANN: I don't know.

(Pause. LAURA assesses him.)

LAURA: If you had to say now, right now, what it is you've got...what would you say?

BOLTZMANN: An inexplicable reaction. *(Then, suddenly, defiant)* But that's certain! There is something happening in that cell. And I as a chemist, as a chemist of forty-five years experience, I can tell you, without equivocation... *(Firm)* ...it is not chemical.

LAURA: *(Challenging)* How do you know that?

BOLTZMANN: Because the heat—

LAURA: The heat is not real.

BOLTZMANN: The heat is most certainly real.

LAURA: The third column?

BOLTZMANN: *(Beat)* The third column—

LAURA: You made the third column up. You didn't do the experiments.

BOLTZMANN: We—

LAURA: Did you do the experiments?

BOLTZMANN: We made assumptions—

LAURA: Based on the first and second columns.

BOLTZMANN: That's right, we—

LAURA: So you didn't do the experiments. *(Her judgement is harsh)* Did you? *(Beat, sharper)* Did you!

(At this, BOLTZMANN *is silent.)*

LAURA: And the first and second columns show no excess heat. The best you got was sixty-two percent. *(Beat)* So how can you say the heat is real?

BOLTZMANN: *(Weak)* Others have reported it. It is not we alone.

LAURA: How can you say the heat is real?

(Pause. BOLTZMANN *is trapped.)*

BOLTZMANN: We can't.

LAURA: You really don't know.

BOLTZMANN: No.

(Pause)

LAURA: So this entire thing...your entire...experiment... could be based on nothing. A series of random events. The meltdown, the... *(She tries to think of others— but can't)* ...nothing.

(Pause)

LAURA: Isn't that right?

(Long pause)

BOLTZMANN: I have a...I cannot explain it to you... but I have a sense...a sense as a scientist...that I have seen something. And I continue to believe it.

LAURA: But don't you need more than that? As a scientist? Don't you need proof?

(A very long pause.)

BOLTZMANN: Yes.

(Beat)

LAURA: And if you don't have it...if you've tried for five years and don't have it...don't you owe the world an explanation?

(At this, BOLTZMANN *looks at her for a long moment, before putting his face in his hands. He then starts to sob. And* LAURA *watches him—until* LEN *suddenly appears— and he too watches* BOLTZMANN. *Then...)*

LEN: What happened?

LAURA: *(Quiet, shaken)* Nothing, I...nothing.

LEN: We have to get out of here.

LAURA: Why, what happened?

LEN: We just got a call.

*(*LEN *goes to* BOLTZMANN.*)*

LAURA: From?

LEN: The White House.

LAURA: Saying?

LEN: They're not meeting us.

LAURA: *(Confused)* They're—

LEN: There's a news conference in Baltimore, or there's going to be...they're tearing us apart. *(Then)* Professor? *(He tries to get* BOLTZMANN *up.)* The press will be here any minute. We gotta get out of here.

LAURA: Len.

LEN: What?

LAURA: *I'm* the press.

(He stops. This last catches his attention.)

LAURA: And I'm already here.

(At this, he simply stares at her.)

LEN: Yeah, well we don't need it to be any worse. *(He then turns back to* BOLTZMANN*)* Professor? We gotta get you out of here.

LAURA: Len.

(And again, he turns to her.)

LAURA: I'm printing this.

LEN: I know.

LAURA: I have to.

LEN: I know!

(Beat)

LAURA: Will you forgive me?

LEN: If I can forgive myself. Come on.

(With that, he brings BOLTZMANN to his feet and the three of them struggle from the room.)

(Blackout. End Scene Seven)

Scene Eight

(Later that week. The University. DEWINDT is at a microphone. His speech, marked by frequent pauses [a politician doing what a politician does best] is prelude to a news conference.)

DEWINDT: I think it's important to put this in context. To put...everything in context. The University had no intention, at *any* point...of putting out misleading information. If we have done so, if we have even inadvertently done so...I take it as my responsibility and I apologize. I apologize to the news media. I apologize to the Congress. And most of all, I apologize to the citizens of our great state. *(Beat)* As to the specifics. *(He take a sip of water.)* As of two P M yesterday, Professor Stevens tendered his resignation. He is no longer affiliated with either our chemistry department of our University. As you all know, of course, Professor Boltzmann was never officially affiliated with our University, but he too has left the

campus and said it is unlikely he will return. And for
this, I can only say—and this is a personal note—that I
am profoundly saddened. Because I have come to know
both Professor Boltzmann *and* Professor Stevens and
think them both fine scientists and fine men. And
parenthetically, to be fair, suspect we have not heard
the last of Cold Fusion. However, we may well have
heard the last of cold fusion at this institution, and for
that I can only say I have very mixed feelings. On the
one hand, I believe these men *have* found something.
I believe there *is* something there. However, I also
believe our institution is not the right place to continue
this research and so as of five P M Monday afternoon,
I am officially closing the Cold Fusion Institute at
University Park. All monies raised on behalf of the
Institute will be returned to their sources, including, I
would emphasize, the five million dollars so generously
awarded by the state legislature at the Governor's
request. Finally...one last comment—and then I'll
take your questions. There are rumors about that
I am thinking of stepping down. These are generally
attached to other rumors suggesting that I used
University monies, secret funds it is alleged, to seed
the fund raising efforts. Well, for the record, let me
just say, *categorically*...neither rumor is true. *(Beat)*
And now I'll take your questions.

(Blackout. End Scene Eight)

Scene Nine

(The lights come up on LEN *and* LAURA. *He is exceedingly
uncomfortable. It is a year later. He is wearing sunglasses.*

LEN: *(Backing away)* No, look, Laura, I can't tell you.

LAURA: Why not?

LEN: I just don't think it's right.

LAURA: Why not!

LEN: Well, actually...I don't even really know.

LAURA: Bullshit.

LEN: I don't, I...I've heard several things.

LAURA: What have you heard?

(This last is asked aggressively—and LEN *looks away. He wants to be elsewhere.)*

LEN: Laura—

LAURA: Len, he's a public figure.

LEN: And it's been a year now.

LAURA: So what?

LEN: So...that lessens things.

LAURA: In what way?

LEN: Laura, I just don't want to be the one.

(Slight pause. She relishes the irony.)

LAURA: Which is rather the way I felt once upon a time.

(Longer pause)

LEN: He's been sick.

LAURA: *(Unmoved)* Uh-huh.

LEN: I'm not joking. He was sick.

LAURA: How sick?

LEN: Very. *(Then)* Actually, I don't know for sure, I...but that's what I heard. Very.

*(*LAURA *doesn't respond. She allows a silence.)*

LEN: Look, what do you want with him?

LAURA: Len, it been a year now. I want to find out what he's up to.

LEN: If he's still a nut?

LAURA: If he still...believes.

(Slight beat)

LEN: Well, like I say—

LAURA: Len, tell me!

LEN: Laura—

LAURA: *(Pleading)* Tell me!

*(She looks at him intensely—and after a moment, suddenly,
LEN spits out an answer—looking away while he is doing so.)*

LEN: The south of France. A Japanese company is
paying them.

LAURA: Where?

LEN: Laura!!

LAURA: What??

(Another moment passes.)

LEN: Outside Nice. But that's it! That's all I know!

LAURA: Thanks.

LEN: Laura!

(This last LEN blurts out as LAURA gets up to leave.)

LAURA: What?

LEN: Can I...call you?

LAURA: *(Caught off)* What?

LEN: Can I...call you?

LAURA: *(Beat)* What for?

LEN: *(Uneasy)* I don't know, I...I don't know.

LAURA: Len, I don't think so.

LEN: Laura—

LAURA: Len, no, really, not... *(Firm)* ...no. *(Then suddenly, she turns out. Calling loudly, plaintively)* Professor Boltzmann! Prof... *(Now in the south of France, she is exasperated, not knowing how to find him.)* Oh, for God—

(Wandering a town square, she suddenly hears an accented voice, crackling from an intercom.)

VOICE: *Je sais pas qui c'est.*

(Dressed in a sun dress and carrying a note pad, LAURA suddenly finds herself next to the intercom, speaking loudly, emphatically, trying to make herself understood.)

LAURA: Professor Boltz-mann. I'm looking for a Professor Bollltzzzmann.

(And again the intercom crackles to life.)

VOICE: *Je parle pas Anglais.*

LAURA: I—

VOICE: *Parlez-vous Francais?*

LAURA: *Parle..? Non...je—*

VOICE: *Excusez-moi.*

(And with that, the voice instantly clicks off. When it does, LAURA practically throws up her hands in frustration.)

LAURA: Oh, for God... *(Then, looking around)* How—

(When suddenly an arrow comes shooting out from an alleyway.)

LAURA: Ah!

(Landing just feet above her, the arrow causes LAURA to fall backwards against a wall, astonished—only to have her mouth fall open in even more astonishment at what she sees next—none other than BOLTZMANN, hair askew, racing out from the alleyway. And instantly she steps forward.)

LAURA: Is that an arrow!!!?

BOLTZMANN: *(Excited)* Yes, it is.

LAURA: Did you shoot it?

BOLTZMANN: From that crossbow, yes.

LAURA: At me????

BOLTZMANN: At...no, of course not!

LAURA: I was standing right there!

BOLTZMANN: You were?

LAURA: You didn't see me?

BOLTZMANN: No...oh, my god.

LAURA: You didn't SEE me???

BOLTZMANN: *(Upset)* I came out and checked. I was out here two minutes ago.

LAURA: Well, I was standing right there!

BOLTZMANN: I'm sorry. I am terribly sorry. *(Beat)* Are you all right?

LAURA: *(Beat, grudging)* I am, yes.

BOLTZMANN: I don't know how that could have happened.

LAURA: It *wasn't* two minutes ago.

BOLTZMANN: *(Beat)* Perhaps it wasn't. I'm sorry.

(Pause)

LAURA: Do you recognize me?

BOLTZMANN: Pardon?

LAURA: Do you know who I am?

BOLTZMANN: I don't, no.

LAURA: I'm Laura Scott.

(She waits for a moment, wondering if he'll remember.)

LAURA: I work for the Post. I met you in Washington.

(Again, a moment passes, and then it's as if a very distant memory is recalled. But BOLTZMAN *makes it seem more than that, as if he remembers her clearly—and happily!)*

BOLTZMANN: Oh. Oh, yes! How *are* you?

LAURA: That's what I've come to ask you.

BOLTZMANN: I'm fine.

LAURA: Are you?

BOLTZMANN: Oh, yes. Wonderful. Couldn't be better. And you?

LAURA: I'm fine.

BOLTZMANN: Well, please, come inside.

LAURA: Do you remember me, Professor?

BOLTZMANN: I do, yes, I... *(But clearly, he doesn't.)*

LAURA: When you were in Washington, when you were testifying. And then just after that.

BOLTZMANN: Yes, I...I recall. *(But again, it's clear he doesn't. It's also clear that he barely remembers testifying. And he doesn't have bad feelings about it.)* Would you like to come in? Or here, tell you what...shall I bring something out? Actually, now that I think of it, I have a pitcher of iced tea in the fridge. Shall I bring that out?

LAURA: Sure.

BOLTZMANN: Here, make yourself comfortable.   .

(And with that, he brings over a stool. He then brings a second stool for himself and immediately exits. Once he's gone, LAURA *takes a moment before going over to the arrow and checking it out. It's at this point that she notices the wire trailing off from its end. As she's inspecting it,* BOLTZMANN *suddenly returns, carrying a pair of glasses and a pitcher.)*

BOLTZMANN: Lead extrusion experiment. Actually a good deal more than that. But it started as lead extrusion.

LAURA: What's that? *(Meaning "what's lead extrusion?")*

BOLTZMANN: It's a joke actually.

(Beat. She crosses back to the stool.)

LAURA: I don't understand.

BOLTZMANN: When my partner was very young... actually not so young, but when he started working with me, he came into my lab on the day I was doing that experiment. Rather like you, in fact. And I thought I would recreate it for him.

(LAURA sits, watching him. Beat.)

LAURA: Interesting.

BOLTZMANN: *(Distracted)* What's that?

LAURA: That you would think to do that...I think is interesting.

(BOLTZMANN laughs slightly.)

LAURA: Is that the only experiment you're doing?

BOLTZMANN: *(Still distracted)* Is...what?

LAURA: Are you doing anything else?

BOLTZMANN: Oh, yes. Oh yes, we're doing several experiments.

LAURA: Can you... *(Taking her time, being careful)* ...talk about them?

BOLTZMANN: Well, for one thing, we're continuing our work on hydrogen research. We've been doing that work for some time.

LAURA: That's...actually why you came to Washington, isn't it?

BOLTZMANN: It is, yes. *(He smiles.)*

LAURA: And? *(Again taking her time)* How's it going?
Can you say?

BOLTZMANN: Quite well, actually. *(He smiles.)*
Quite well.

LAURA: Can you elaborate?

*(As she says this, she studies him...wondering if he's being
purposely evasive.)*

BOLTZMANN: Put it this way...we're going to have a
MAJOR announcement in a very short period of time.
Beyond that I can't say.

(Beat)

LAURA: I see.

BOLTZMANN: But this I CAN say. About my experiment
this afternoon. It's going to be quite something if I can
pull it off. The only question is...can I pull it off? *(And
with that, he gets to his feet.)*

BOLTZMANN: Do you understand what I'm doing here?

(LAURA shakes her head.)

BOLTZMANN: I'm shooting this arrow...from that
crossbow... *(He points.)* ...to this spot right here.
(He points to the wall.)

BOLTZMANN: If I hit this spot...a circuit will be
completed and a new hydrogen diffusion cell will
begin charging. *(Beat)* The only question is...can I
pull it off? *(And with that, he starts off.)*

BOLTZMANN: I have an idea.

*(He then exits, and LAURA looks after him. Her brow
furrowed, she watches as he grabs the crossbow offstage,
and returns with it.)*

BOLTZMANN: *(Entering)* See this, I think, was my mistake. Bad angle. I have it out here...I line it up out here... *(He sets the crossbow down, facing it towards the wall.)*

BOLTZMANN: I don't think I'll have any problem. *(He then starts to aim the contraption.)* What do you think?

(LAURA continues to stare at him—not answering. Till finally, BOLTZMANN looks up.)

BOLTZMANN: Any idea?

LAURA: *(Beat, vacant)* I don't know.

BOLTZMANN: *(Playfully)* Well, you must have faith in me.

LAURA: Professor! *(This last she says more impatiently, forcefully—more forcefully than she meant to.)* Are you... do you have any idea why I'm here?

BOLTZMANN: To talk to me... *(He takes a moment.)* ...about cold fusion, I should think.

LAURA: *(Beat)* Yes.

(Beat)

BOLTZMANN: Well... *(His voice is gentle, inviting.)* ...talk.

(LAURA stares at him—not sure how to take this. Then...)

LAURA: You say you're going to have a major announcement. What's it going to be?

BOLTZMANN: *(Beat)* I'm not sure I'm ready to say.

LAURA: Can you just tell me the area?

(Again, he takes a moment.)

BOLTZMANN: Heat. It will concern excess heat.

LAURA: Have you gotten any?

BOLTZMANN: We have. Yes. Ten times the amount as last year.

LAURA: Have you gotten neutrons?

BOLTZMANN: No. Just the heat. *(Beat)* And I should note, in the year intervening, there have been fifteen other labs that have ALSO gotten heat.

LAURA: So you're...what do you think that means?

BOLTZMANN: It means the same as it always has. That we don't know what we've got. We just know that we HAVE something. *(After a moment, he then smiles, turning back to the crossbow.)* But here...we know exactly what we've got. We just have to get there. *(And with that, he crosses from the crossbow to the wall, looking back when he gets there.)* Now I didn't tell you one other thing. The most important element. In addition to powering the cell, there is also a small wire running to an attached light bulb. If I hit the bulls-eye, in other words, it will not only ignite the cell... it will also turn on a light on the second floor. So keep your eyes upstairs. *(He comes back.)* And cross your fingers. *(Again he finds himself behind the crossbow.)* One final thing. A word about the crossbow. It was designed as a powerful, precision-guided weapon in the latter half of the twelfth century. It was not, however, designed to do what we're trying here. The result is that we may have to do this more than once. *(He turns back.)* Let's hope not. *(Then)* Ready?

(LAURA nods her head.)

BOLTZMANN: Three...two...one—

STEVENS: What is SHE doing here? *(He comes charging in from the side.)*

BOLTZMANN: Parker, I'm—

STEVENS: Would you mind telling me that?

BOLTZMANN: I'm trying to conduct an experiment, Parker.

LAURA: I'm here to interview the Professor.

STEVENS: About what?

LAURA: About—

BOLTZMANN: Would you two *mind... (He is clearly put out.)* ...conducting this conversation when I'm finished?

(STEVENS remains on LAURA.)

STEVENS: Did he tell you?

LAURA: Tell me what?

STEVENS: What we've got. What we're getting rather. Ten *times* the heat we were getting last year!

LAURA: He told me that, yes.

STEVENS: Will you print it?

LAURA: I'll print that he said it.

STEVENS: You'll...did you hear that, Otto?

BOLTZMANN: Parker, I'm trying—

STEVENS: She'll print that you "said" it. It's the same thing as always.

BOLTZMANN: I don't care!

(This last is said sharply. So sharply that STEVENS looks at BOLTZMANN—noticing, for the first time, the crossbow.)

STEVENS: What are you doing?

BOLTZMANN: *(Impatient)* An experiment.

STEVENS: Lead extrusion?

BOLTZMANN: Something different. *(Beat, impatient)* Will you watch?

STEVENS: *(Beat)* Sure.

(BOLTZMANN turns back to the crossbow.)

BOLTZMANN: It's actually a combination of things.
Lead extrusion...and our more recent endeavor.
(Beat) Perhaps an interesting result. *(Beat)* Ready?

(LAURA nods.)

BOLTZMANN: Let's do it.

*(And with that, he suddenly lets fly with the bolt which
streaks across the stage, slamming, brightly, into the wall
opposite. BOLTZMANN studies it for a short moment before
turning to LAURA.)*

BOLTZMANN: Did it hit?

LAURA: *(Confused)* What?

BOLTZMANN: The bulls-eye? Did it hit? *(He is excited.)*

LAURA: Yes. *(She is walking over.)*

BOLTZMANN: And? Can you see the light?

LAURA: *(Confused)* Can...

BOLTZMANN: The light upstairs?

LAURA: Oh. No, I... *(She cranes her neck, looking upstairs)*
...I... *(Then suddenly)* Oh, wait a minute. *(Suddenly,
excited)* In the window, there, I see a reflection!

BOLTZMANN: You see the light?

LAURA: Yes!

STEVENS: What light?

BOLTZMANN: On the second floor. There's a light.
I wasn't sure you could see it.

LAURA: I can! I can see the reflection!

STEVENS: Which means what?

BOLTZMANN: What?

STEVENS: *(Caught up in the excitement)* What does the
light mean?

(BOLTZMANN *turns to* STEVENS, *a smile on his face—taking his time.*)

BOLTZMANN: It means we have a chance.

(STEVENS *is mystified.*)

STEVENS: What?

(BOLTZMANN *repeats, his eyebrows arched, a smile still creasing his face.*)

BOLTZMANN: It means we have a chance.

LAURA: Could—

BOLTZMANN: *(To* STEVENS, *pressing him)* Do you understand why?

STEVENS: *(Still mystified)* No.

BOLTZMANN: Because we remain experimenters. Because we remain excited. Because—

LAURA: Professor—

STEVENS: *(Reaching out, protective)* Otto, let's—

BOLTZMANN: Don't touch me!

(This last BOLTZMANN *screams, his outburst catching the two others off-guard.)*

BOLTZMANN: I am trying to explain something to you. And to you as well. *(This last he says to* LAURA, *before turning back to* STEVENS.)*

BOLTZMANN: About what it is we are doing here. And why we still have a chance. Because we remain excited. Because we are experimenters in science and we remain excited. And so long as we remain excited, so long as we are *willing* to investigate...we still have a chance. It's only when we stop having fun, when we no longer see the pleasure of firing a crossbow into a silly, metal target...a stupid, childish, meaningless trick...that we lose all hope of advancing. *(Again he turns to* LAURA.*)* Do you see?

LAURA: *(Hesitant, dubious)* I...do a bit, yes.

BOLTZMANN: *(Beat)* Well, I'll let Parker explain the rest.

(And with that BOLTZMANN *exits—and a long silence exists between* LAURA *and* STEVENS. *Then, finally...)*

LAURA: Is he...?

STEVENS: He's what he is. *(Slight beat)* What you made him.

LAURA: I...didn't make him anything, Professor. I merely reported what he'd done.

STEVENS: With charity? *(Beat)* With kindness? With hope?

LAURA: With objectivity.

*(*STEVENS *chuckles bitterly.)*

LAURA: Why do you laugh?

STEVENS: Because it's all so simple to you. And so wrong. Did it ever... *(He thinks for a moment.)* ...no, never mind.

LAURA: What?

(He looks her over a moment.)

STEVENS: Did it ever occur to you...that even if we were wrong, even if we made TERRIBLE mistakes...we may still have found something of value?

LAURA: *(Suddenly unsure)* No.

STEVENS: No. It wouldn't. Because you're not a scientist. If you *were* a scientist... *(Getting angry)* ...you would realize some of the greatest work, the greatest advances, the most *valuable* experiments...were those that opened up fields of study without proving their outcomes. And that's what HE has done. He may have been wrong...but he showed us where to look. And that alone is worth our thanks.

LAURA: But he cheated. Too. Didn't he? I mean—

STEVENS: Everyone cheats.

LAURA: Ev—

STEVENS: Everyone cheats! I mean, my God, what the fuck do you think science is? Do you think it's this pure realm? Do you think it's this place where people stop being human? Everyone cheats! And not just the people who are wrong, either. The people who are honored. Isaac Newton cheated. Millikan cheated. Dalton. Mendel. Gregor Mendel, for God's sakes. The father of modern genetics. He fixed his data. It is commonly recognized that he fixed his data. There was a paper in 1936 that proved that very fact. So what should we do with that fact? Should we string the man up? Should we reduce him to tears? Or should we honor him, as the world has honored Mendel, as the world has *honored* Millikan... *(Furious, practically screaming)* ...he was awarded the Nobel Prize, for God's sake!...for the great work they have done.

(A long moment passes. LAURA *is silent.)*

STEVENS: Everyone cheats. But not everyone has the vision...and courage...and tenacity...to take a fresh look at the world.

(Pause)

STEVENS: You have taken a man who has within him all that is most wondrous...most noble...most exalted... about humanity...and reduced him to nothing. *(Beat)* And for that you should be ashamed.

(Another moment passes.)

LAURA: *(Crushed)* I...

BOLTZMANN: I don't think she should be ashamed.
(*At this, he again emerges from inside.*)

BOLTZMANN: I think she would be thanked. For coming once more to see me. And ask questions. And take an interest in my work. (*Beat*) Not many are any more. And so I thank her for being one who is.

(*Pause.* LAURA *is very confused—and moved.*)

LAURA: I wanted... (*Beat*) ...I came here to see if you still believed. If you still were working. And you are. And despite myself...despite all I believe...I am glad of it.

(BOLTZMANN *smiles. Then, after a beat...*)

BOLTZMANN: Come. Come inside. Join us for a meal. Will you join us?

LAURA: (*Beat*) Yes.

BOLTZMANN: Come. (*He tilts his head.*) Parker?

(*And with that, he and* STEVENS *exit—leaving* LAURA *alone. Still stunned by all that has happened, she starts to move when suddenly her eyes falls on the arrow still stuck in the wall. Going over to it, she looks up at the light and removes the arrow, causing the light to go out. And for a moment she simple stands there, arrow in hand, looking up. And then, on impulse, she buries the arrow once again into the wall— so that the light once again comes on. And then she backs up to take one final look...as the lights, once again, fade to black.*)

(*End Scene Nine*)

END OF PLAY

Cold Fusion Cell

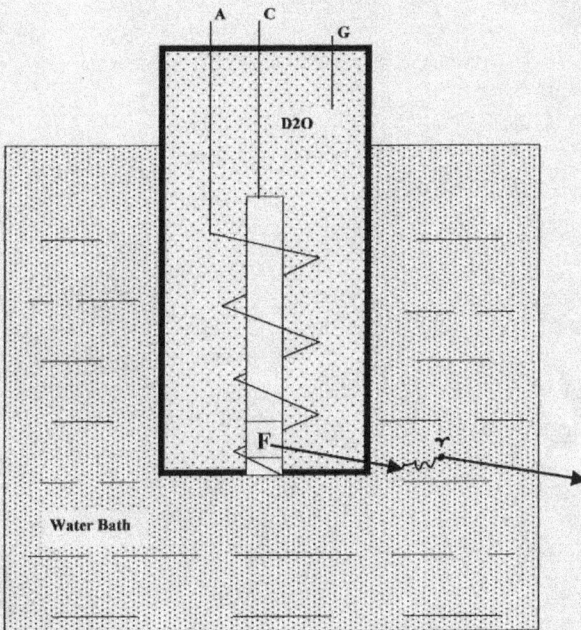

A = Platinum anode

C = Palladium cathode

G = "Heavy" water (D2O)

When fusion occurs inside the cathode, at F, a neutron is emitted which enters the water bath and is captured at γ, emitting a gamma ray of energy at 2.2 MeV.

www.ingramcontent.com/pod-product-compliance
Lightning Source LLC
Chambersburg PA
CBHW052117090426
42741CB00009B/1848